D1033042

WORDSWORTH AND COLERIDGE

Wordsworth

AND

Coleridge

A Study of their Literary Relations in 1801-1802

BY

WILLIAM HEATH

CLARENDON PRESS · OXFORD
1970

Oxford University Press, Ely House, London W. 1

GLASGOW   NEW YORK   TORONTO   MELBOURNE   WELLINGTON
CAPE TOWN   SALISBURY   IBADAN   NAIROBI   DAR ES SALAAM   LUSAKA   ADDIS ABABA
BOMBAY   CALCUTTA   MADRAS   KARACHI   LAHORE   DACCA
KUALA LUMPUR   SINGAPORE   HONG KONG   TOKYO

© OXFORD UNIVERSITY PRESS 1970

821.71
H 438 w

141494

MOUNT UNION COLLEGE
LIBRARY

PRINTED IN GREAT BRITAIN
AT THE UNIVERSITY PRESS
ABERDEEN

TO MEL

Preface

I SHALL try to tell a story about the activities of six people, three of them extraordinary, during the year from November 1801 to October 1802. As I do so, I realize that any magnification of biographical details in order to yield a sense of life is distortion, that no man's life was conducted in the words and records that happen to survive him, and that no biographer's order can be more than shapes and forms for which he has some predilection. But the details for the persons that comprise my subject are temptingly full, and the literary result of whatever did actually happen during that year is demonstrably important, if poetry and poets matter. During these twelve months William Wordsworth and his sister Dorothy, Mary Hutchinson (soon to become William's wife) and her sister Sara, Samuel Taylor Coleridge and his wife Sara all adopted directions which they were to follow for the rest of their lives.

Simply as a story about interesting people the subject is compelling. Probably for no other group of similarly intelligent and articulate people do such full records exist that show the impingement of one life on another, and the relation of each to the group they form and the world in which that group exists. In letters, journals and poems, people are seen doing and saying things to one another of such significance that they alter other things that are said and done, just as they might in any seriously dramatic novel. The words they speak repeatedly reveal what Lawrence called the central concern of any important fiction—the relation between the self and the circumambient universe. Their sense of haunting destinies and enabling freedoms are constantly perceptible in what they say to one another.

But this is only one justification for retelling the story. The more important fact is that during the activities that can be reconstructed for this year, two of the greatest of English poets composed some of England's finest autobiographical poems.

Lives are there to be seen, however inaccurately, but the art toward which the lives were shaped and which in turn shaped them survives both as attempt and successful achievement. If the literary historian has ever been given adequate material from which to construct some statement about possible relations between art and life, it is in the records and poems of this year. Of course it is a subject that has already attracted more than a few students of literature, and the present essay is a new order rather than a new beginning. Every man, contemplating the work of another, must speak for himself.

To tell the story I see here I shall try to use every art and every source I can respect or justify. Some of these sources can offer no real reason for dispute, except for my errors in fact and judgement: the poems, and some of their early versions, are present both as manuscripts and as revised printed texts. And a great many letters survive in which the characters of this—now—fiction speak to and about one another. More privately, Dorothy Wordsworth's *Journal*, whose assumed audience is sometimes public but usually private, is a record of what one person saw as a chronological ordering of the continually present moments of her life. And Coleridge's notebooks, recording trivia and meaning in a manner as private and chaotic as a shopping list or a dream, are an almost random collection of pencil marks of a kind any man might have happened to scratch in one place in a year, but that only one man could and did. These documents, in their varying degrees of comprehensibility and importance, are the hard stuff of existence, the polished surface of the past through which any reader can catch glimpses of what finally may be no more than his own reflection. But the words and things looked at are there, separable from their uses but meaningless without them.

To move from record to narrative is the necessary and uncertain next step. We can know, to some extent, what a man said, wrote or did; we can know what he has read, whom he has seen, what illnesses he has suffered. But such knowledge cannot by itself make us care or understand. His projected sense of his own destiny, the intensity of the sufferings and satisfactions of his own life, the whole continuity that comprises his identity—all these remain as obscure and untrustworthy as a biographer's own interest. I hope I shall not pretend otherwise, but I shall not hesitate to make a story, justifying all my constructions by what they can add to the order of a statement whose final truth, as with any narrative, is judged by its reader. My motive, it should be said once, is selfish: to be the builder of another context within which great art can be read.

Acknowledgements

THIS essay began in Oxford in 1963. For assistance in making research and writing possible, I should like to thank the President and Trustees of Amherst College, who granted a Trustee Fellowship for 1962–3, a research grant to supplement it, and a sabbatical leave to complete the work in 1967–8. This second leave was additionally aided by a grant from the Penrose Fund of the American Philosophical Society.

I am especially indebted to the late Professor Herbert Davis for his many kindnesses during the first stay in England. The staffs of the Bodleian Library, the English Faculty Library in Oxford, the Reading and Manuscript Rooms of the British Museum, the University of London Library, and the London Library all gave generous hospitality and assistance. For several visits to the Dove Cottage Library I am particularly grateful to Miss Nesta Clutterbuck, its librarian, and to Mrs. Mary Moorman and Professor Basil Willey, who gave their permission as Trustees.

At home, the services of the Amherst College Library—and its reference librarians Floyd Merritt and E. Porter Dickinson—have been indispensable, as have the libraries of Smith and Mount Holyoke colleges. Miss K. Backhouse, in London, and Mrs. James Crosson, in Amherst, typed most of the manuscript.

Jonathan Bishop first told me how interesting Wordsworth could be, and conversations with Richard Haven and George Whalley have brought me unearned knowledge of Coleridge. My present and past colleagues at Amherst, and many students, have contributed more than they know. My debt to my wife is irredeemable.

Contents

Note on Editions and Abbreviations

QUOTATIONS from the letters and journals of Coleridge and the Wordsworths are usually identified by date, rather than by page or number used in standard editions, because a revised edition of the Wordsworth letters has begun to appear, the Coleridge letters will be published in the collected edition, and a new edition of Dorothy Wordsworth's *Journal* soon will be made. Notebook entries for Coleridge are identified by their numbers in Kathleen Coburn's edition, which is unlikely to be superseded in the predictable future. Texts of early Wordsworth letters are taken from the de Selincourt Oxford edition, as revised (1967) by C. L. Shaver; texts of Wordsworth poems (except where modified by manuscript evidence) are from the five-volume Oxford edition, as edited by de Selincourt and Helen Darbishire; both the de Selincourt two-volume and the Darbishire World Classics editions are used for the quotations from Dorothy Wordsworth's *Journal*, and most of these have been checked against the manuscripts. The texts of the Coleridge letters come mostly from E. L. Grigg's edition, and of the poems from E. H. Coleridge's two-volume Oxford edition, except where modified by manuscript readings.

The following abbreviations are used:

BP   Robert Anderson, ed., *A Complete Edition of the Poets of Great Britain*, 13 vols., 1795.

NB   *The Notebooks of Samuel Taylor Coleridge*, ed. K. Coburn, vol. I (1794–1804), London, 1957.

DWJ   *The Journals of Dorothy Wordsworth*, ed. de Selincourt (London, 1941, 2 vols.) or ed. Darbishire (Oxford, 1958).

CHAPTER I

The Tender Fiction

WHEN Wordsworth, in his 'Essay upon Epitaphs', speaks out for the right of rustic engravers to 'personate the deceased, and represent him as speaking from his own tombstone', he implicitly asserts the permanent task and the essential freedom of all poets and tellers of tales:

The departed Mortal is introduced telling you himself that his pains are gone; that a state of rest is come; and he conjures you to weep for him no longer. .... By this tender fiction, the survivors bind themselves to a sedater sorrow, and employ the intervention of the imagination in order that the reason may speak her own language earlier than she would otherwise have been enabled to do (*Prose Works*, II, 39).

And it is the function and privilege of this tender fiction, this 'shadowy interposition', to subvert without contravening the motive and care and fastidiousness of the reason, because the aim of the epitaph maker, perhaps too the poet, is not communication but composition. The Ancient Mariner, after all, required only the meagerest audience, impatient and uncomprehending, that he might set his own life in order, bind himself to a sedater terror. In poems, prose, letters, reading and conversation, Wordsworth and Coleridge persistently return to the question of how a poet's obligations define his audience; and their work of 1802, culminating for Coleridge in the final version of 'Dejection: An Ode', for Wordsworth in 'Resolution and Independence', can be seen as parts of a dialogue that makes any serious poet's dilemma far more complex than the choice between self-expression and communication.

It was Coleridge, characteristically (for no poet was ever less given to heeding his own advice), who repeatedly reminded himself that communication ought to be possible even in the most unlikely circumstances: whether 'endeavouring to make the infinitely beloved Darling [Sara Hutchinson] understand all my knowledge', or defining the passion of friendship as the result of the disappointed desire for 'the unspeakable comfort' of being *understood*. For Wordsworth a poet's isolation from explicit language was, because it was recognized, less a threat than an opportunity. Defending 'The Idiot Boy' in a letter of June 1802 (to John Wilson), Wordsworth replies, at first with assurance, that the poet can only hope to please one audience, 'human nature'. But, less assuredly, he locates human nature. It is found when a poet begins by 'stripping [his] own heart naked' and habitually looks out of himself 'towards men who lead the simplest lives'. This accomplished, the poet has a chance not only to give pleasure but also 'new compositions of feeling'. Finally much is made possible but nothing is transferred. Poetry enables but does not award its reader. The poet, like the child, the idiot, the king, speaks for himself and entrusts to his reader the obligation of understanding. An almost regal independence informs the tone of most of the sentences to Wilson, and here, as in the Preface to *Lyrical Ballads*, such assurance in a man still forty years away from being Poet Laureate is remarkable.

A good many years later, in his note to a description of the dignified man ('Free as the sun, and lonely as the sun') in book III of *The Excursion* Wordsworth first quoted the following note from Gilbert's *The Hurricane* and called it 'one of the finest passages of modern English prose'. Such an extravagant evaluation is understandable for a statement that brings together coherently though abstractly the importance to the educated man of imagination, childlike independence and regal self-reliance. Gilbert (in 1795) deplored the artificial man who seeks to 'extend his sphere' by embracing the minutiae of London with 'barren and inhuman pruriency', contrasting this intellectual sensualist with the Man of Mind who 'contemplates, from a sudden promontory, the distant, vast Pacific—and feels himself a freeman in this vast theatre' with an 'exaltation [that] is not less than imperial' and because it is imperial can afford to be gentle:

He becomes at once a child and a king. His mind is in himself; from hence he argues, and from hence he acts, and he argues unerringly, and acts magisterially; his mind in himself is also in his God; and therefore he loves, and therefore he soars.

This serene confidence, of course, tempts charges of fatuousness and smugness, the complementary vices of child and king, and these charges are granted by Coleridge in his despair at Wordsworth's pendantry. 'Always to look at the superficies of Objects for the purpose of taking Delight in their Beauty, & sympathy with their real or imagined Life,' he writes about Wordsworth in his Notebook in 1803, 'is as deleterious to the Health & manhood of Intellect, as always to be peering & unravelling Contrivances may be to the simplicity of the affections, the grandeur & unity of the Imagination' (*NB*, 1616). Coleridge's scorn, reminiscent of that he directed against himself in 'Dejection' ('Haply by abstruse Research to steal / From my own Nature, all the Natural man'), suggests a yearning for, and a fundamental distrust of, the confidence of genius, its ability or assumed prerogative to reshape and alter in accommodating the world to the self's overriding purpose. Wordsworth himself, not a steam engine, may well have been the subject of the exchange between Wordsworth and Coleridge reported by Dorothy during their tour in Scotland:

When we drew nearer [to the mining village in the Nith Valley] we saw, coming out of the side of the building, a large machine or lever, in appearance like a great forge-hammer, as we supposed for raising water out of the mines. It heaved upwards once in half a minute with a slow motion, and seemed to rest to take breath at the bottom, its motion being accompanied with a sound between a groan and *jike*. There would have been something in this object very striking in any place, as it was impossible not to invest the machine with some faculty of intellect; it seemed to have made the first step from brute matter to life and purpose, showing its progress by great power. William made a remark to this effect, and Coleridge observed that it was like a giant with one idea . . . (*DWJ*, I, 207–8).

Probably Coleridge's reputation suffers undeservedly because of the full evidence of his doubts and intentions. He is by far the best example of his own description (in *The Friend*) of an author who must tune his harp 'in the hearing of those, who are to understand its after harmonies; the foundation stones of his edifice must lie open to common view, or his friends will hesitate to trust themselves beneath his roof'. Yet the often coy alternations of openness and secrecy in the Notebooks and letters, even the elaborate monograms and pseudonyms, seen together with his life-long inability to complete literary projects and his later accusations of plagiarism against Wordsworth, appear as adolescent as Wordsworth's serenity appears prematurely elderly or his simplicity childish. Whether or not the reader accepts alternatives like Bronowski's ('... we find Wordsworth smug and Coleridge lively; or we find Wordsworth sterling and Coleridge shoddy'), Bronowski is right in claiming that both poets have in effect forced their readers to render judgements that are more psychological than literary by challenging the 'right of poetry to have *any* standard' (*The Poet's Defence*, Cambridge, 1939, pp. 129–31). Caught in the labyrinth of their own new language about the relation between the self and its circumambient universe, the two poets largely restrict themselves to this way of talking about poetic success and failure. As Bronowski shows, Coleridge, with far more occasions for grieving about failure, was never as desperate or as successful as Wordsworth, for whom loss of interest—roughly called nature—meant loss of life (pp. 157–61). Coleridge, but not Wordsworth, could be made a thinker by his imagination's failure, because order, not the thing ordered, was his goal and standard—as Keats implies by using Coleridge's mode as the antithesis of negative capability. But in any event, if a poet attempts to reconcile the fixed self to the fluid universe, or to accommodate a universe of show to the fluid self, if he chooses Wordsworth's mode or Coleridge's, he assumes an immense responsibility.

He must go on explaining, to himself and to his readers, what he is doing, apologizing often for his failure either to make their lives or his own sublime. Composition becomes an activity within which poems can often appear as by-products, progress reports, steps taken toward the achievement of something more in the life of the poet or the reader.

So the exact terms used to differentiate these two poets are not always important. It is a matter of record that both found the process of writing exhausting to the health and spirits. Dorothy Wordsworth explains (to Mary Hutchinson in 1801) that her brother is made even more ill by revision than by original composition, and her *Journal* for the spring of 1802 refers repeatedly to fits of headache and fatigue brought on by writing. Though her language for personal feeling is rarely extravagant, one of William's struggles with what became the first book of *The Excursion* results simply in a marginal note saying 'Disaster Pedlar'. Coleridge, observed in the process of composition only by himself, has left even more vivid evidence of his struggles: in the incoherencies, ciphers, confessions, complaints and syntactical triumphs of the Notebooks; or in the violence of the language he uses to describe the secondary imagination that struggles and fuses. The act of writing was for both poets an expense of spirit, a necessity, and a burden.

Accounts of the related efforts of the two poets in the spring of 1802 have been given before, and made into tales of conflict and resolution. If only because literary history records no other fruitful confrontation of will and talent so fully documented, so exactly located in time and place, it is a story that should be told once again. In the less than twenty weeks between March 19th, when Coleridge arrived at Town End in Grasmere, and July 29th, when Wordsworth and his sister left Grasmere for Calais, Wordsworth had written at least twice as many poems as appeared in the whole *Lyrical Ballads* of 1798, including 'The Rainbow,' 'Resolution and Independence', and a half of 'Intimations of Immortality'. Including the considerable work done on *The Prelude* and *The Excursion* during this period, the four-month effort was the last great period of concentrated and artistically successful composition in a career that was to continue for forty-eight years more.

Coleridge's successive (and progressive) rewritings of 'Dejection', apparently his only major effort at poetic composition during the same period, was even more conclusively a final successful effort in his own career as a poet. Only a quarter of the sixty poems that appeared in *Sybilline Leaves* in 1817 were

written after the summer of 1802. In the eighty years remaining
for both poets, neither wrote enough, or well enough, to earn
him the position in English literary history he has today. Of
course nothing can explain the greatness of these poems at this
moment, though some reasons for their number and nature may
be suggested. But one can speculate profitably about why the
prolific moment, for both poets, was not extended. The self-
conscious discovery of the difference between composition and
communication can, by pointing the way to a solution of an
intellectual problem, destroy the source of confusion and mystery
from which a poet writes. Everything suggests that such an
apprehension, for both poets, took place in the spring of 1802. As
Wordsworth says, with a perhaps embarrassed allusion to the
tenuousness of the poet's craft, the intervention of the imagination
is both shadowy and tender.

A poem like 'The Rainbow' is useful in identifying one form of
the imagination's shadowy and tender intervention, and can help
to remove any suspicion that the tender fiction, in poetry if not
in epitaphs, is simply pretence and the assertion of fantasy,
though it may partake of both. The vocabulary and syntax of this
short poem are spare, utterly simple, almost totally mysterious:

> My heart leaps up when I behold
> A Rainbow in the sky:
> So was it when my life began;
> So is it now I am a Man;
> So be it when I shall grow old,
>   Or let me die!
> The Child is Father of the Man;
> And I could wish my days to be
> Bound each to each by natural piety.

No time is specified, no events are particularized, and the shifts of
tense result almost in contradiction. A generalized assertion,
extended in time, becomes a wish: but the tone, informed with the
sort of serenity that Coleridge for one was justly quick to resent,
denies that any retreat, any dramatic qualification, has taken
place—So, So, So. However, the persistence of a response is not
inevitable proof of a continuity, certainly not one that so easily

earns the title of Natural Piety. Indeed the discovery of an earlier
version of the poem, sent to Sara Hutchinson that spring, reveals
that the triumphant tone of the last line is at best a matter of
rhetoric, at worst a rather shoddy ambiguity. In its earlier version
the poem, more forthrightly called 'Extempore', concludes:

> And I should wish that all my days may be
> Bound each to each by natural piety.

The assertion of Leavis, Empson and others that a characteristic
Wordsworthian mode is to make the nicety of statement appear
to demonstrate the inevitability of an untenable conclusion has
here its plainest justification. Something, we need not call it
imagination, has enabled the reason to speak her own language
earlier than she would otherwise have been able to do. Wordsworth may well have been 'haunted with altering "The Rainbow"' two months after he composed it, and his pencilled
marginal note on MS. M—'Perhaps boyish years instead of life I
mean remembered life'—reflects his continuing concern with its
clarity.[1] Since the alterations of late May, by which he was
haunted, were presumably included in the version sent to Sara,
the original poem in March must have been very unsure indeed.

But in spite of implicit doubts about the rhetoric of the poem,
Wordsworth seems to have been quite clear about the vocabulary
he was using. The generalizations, the refusal to specify in any
way the nature of the feeling named, express at once his confidence
in his language and a recognition that it cannot specify further
and remain true. Concerned always with extending his own
powers as a poet, Wordsworth recognized at the same time a
limit to the possibilities for all poets. Only a few weeks earlier
Wordsworth had read out to his sister Ben Jonson's 'beautiful
poem on Love', presumably 'Why I Write Not of Love', a

---

[1] Manuscript M in the Wordsworth Library at Grasmere is a bound volume of
poems written after 1800 and before March 1804, transcribed by Dorothy
Wordsworth and Sara Hutchinson. This manuscript, the manuscript anthology
made by Sara Hutchinson in 1802 and called *Sara's Poets* (now also at Dove
Cottage), and the Longman (Meyerstein) manuscript for the 1807 *Poems* (now in
the British Museum) are the most frequent sources for the textual variants indicated in this and in subsequent poems.

whimsical defence for not having attempted an impossible subject. And a dispute about Jonson occupied both poets on the evening Coleridge arrived at Grasmere. Although not much can be said to link Jonson's very different poem with 'The Rainbow', both poets, in confronting unresolvable perplexity, do respond characteristically—Wordsworth of course relying on generality rather than wit. Both poems, facing the unspeakable, comprise more release than clarification.

'The Rainbow', in part because of these inadequacies, typifies most economically the perplexities facing Wordsworth as a man and as a poet during the spring of 1802. It is a transparent account of a supposedly intense perception, the attempt to organize that perception, and the failure finally to control it. When one looks only at the poems Wordsworth had written before the spring of 1802, 'The Rainbow' looks surprisingly different in the intensity of its autobiographical concern, in the economy of its confrontation with a perception barely defined, and in the desperation of its conclusion. Most surprising of all, perhaps, is the fact that the poem itself offers no reason why a reader should attend to it. If one reads it with interest, it is because of one's pre-existing interest in the poet who wrote it. Among his earlier poems, primarily those that had appeared in the two editions of *Lyrical Ballads*, only 'Tintern Abbey' and the Lucy poems are so explicitly auto-biographical, and in the first of these the reader is given enough information to realize who is speaking, and why he should listen. Of course Wordsworth had begun *The Prelude*, its form represented only briefly in the second edition of *Lyrical Ballads* by 'Nutting', at Goslar in 1799, but that was part of a single-minded major task, not a sudden outburst having no particular reference to what had been written the day before or the day after. The strangeness of 'The Rainbow' is partly found in its isolation from a project, and the undeliberateness of its apparent motive.

And 'The Rainbow' did inaugurate a new concern. When it is set beside the poems written after it in the spring of 1802, it almost disappears in its typicality, and its last three lines blend so neatly as the epigraph to the 'Immortality' Ode (from the edition of 1815 onwards) that it is difficult to remember they have

a separate existence. Certainly the appearance of 'The Rainbow'
in the *Poems* of 1807, in the section called 'Moods of my own
Mind', is hardly startling, and Wordsworth there did not even
bother to give it a title. By the time of the edition of 1815, where
it first heads the section of 'Poems referring to the Period of
Childhood', it again in effect serves as an epigraph. In every
edition from 1815 to 1840, 'The Rainbow' (called 'My heart
leaps up') and the Ode are printed as the first and last poems,
framing the Collected Works.

Even though 'The Rainbow' can never be called a major poem,
it had great usefulness to Wordsworth, and to his readers, as a key
poem. The new poetic concern it initiates is as typically Wordsworthian as any of the *Lyrical Ballads*. Its methods can, by contrast, indicate the modes used in far more important poems such
as the 'Immortality' Ode and 'Resolution and Independence'. And
its composition at this particular time allows a biographer to
create a moment in Wordsworth's career that can be seen as a
crucial and significant redefinition of the uses of poetry. When
Wordsworth submitted for publication the poems that were to
make up the 1807 volume, he included with them an advertisement in which he described the short poems, most of them written
in 1802, as 'chiefly composed to refresh my mind during the
progress of a work of length and labour, in which I have been for
some time engaged; and to furnish me with employment when I
had not resolution to apply myself to that work'. Although the
tone of the advertisement is entirely public, the claim and excuse
that the poems are primarily 'refreshment' is misleading. Clearly
the circumstances of their composition suggest that 'refreshment'
meant more than merely keeping agile the mind and pen of the
author of *The Recluse*.

The argument of the chapters that follow is that 'refreshment'
is Wordsworth's name for his search for authenticity—a style,
a statement, and a way of regarding his own life that reconciles
experience to expectation and gives it permanent form in the
language of reason. For at least eight years Wordsworth wrote and
rewrote essentially the same poem, seeking the new composition
of feeling that would render sane and permanent his response to

the story of Margaret, the encounter with the discharged soldier, the realization of having crossed the Alps, the ascent of Snowdon, the frantic deadness of London, the suppressed ambition of life at Grasmere, the loss of exuberant vision, the changing circumstances of his own life—and all the Spots of Time that return, bidden or unbidden, to renovate, nourish and repair. It is the conclusion of this argument that in the writing of 'Resolution and Independence' in the spring of 1802 Wordsworth most successfully used his knowledge of poetry's possibilities and the resources of his own imagination to achieve this authenticity. The audience then was small but complex: writing in his own voice to create permanence and a sanity meant using, understanding and finally rejecting the rich authority of the sensibilities of his sister and Coleridge, both of whom implicitly counselled attitudes that meant despair or surrender. Rejecting communication for composition, he became one of those whom

> the enduring and the transient both
> Serve to exalt; they build up greatest things
> From least suggestions; ever on the watch,
> Willing to work and to be wrought upon,
> They need not extraordinary calls
> To rouse them; in a world of life they live,
> By sensible impressions not enthralled,
> But by their quickening impulse made more prompt
> To hold fit converse with the spiritual world,
> And with the generations of mankind
> Spread over time, past, present, and to come
> Age after age, till Time shall be no more.
> (*The Prelude* (1850), XIV, 100–11)

CHAPTER II

Home at Grasmere

(i)

TO SEE March and April 1802 as an important period, it is useful
to go back some months and consider the period of inactivity
which preceded Wordsworth's sudden activity. His decision to
settle at Grasmere after he and Dorothy had returned from Germany in 1799 was occasioned by economic necessity but supported by a vision of a new life. As the 1800 draft of 'Home at
Grasmere', and, later, the opening lines of *The Prelude* show,
Wordsworth found a metaphor for his situation at this moment
in Milton's account of the expulsion of Adam and Eve from Eden
at the end of *Paradise Lost*. The lines in *The Prelude* made the
choice explicit and singular—'The earth is all before me'—but
'Home at Grasmere' in less Miltonic vocabulary more directly
invokes the situation of *Paradise Lost*. The speaker in this poem is
like Adam before and after the Fall, seeking both the paradise within and that without, making solitude into companionship and
companionship into solitude, arguing for wise passivity and
violent action, placing Grasmere apart from one real world and
at the centre of another. In these ambiguous redefinitions of
Grasmere, the means by which Wordsworth reconsiders his own
situation and projects a future, can be found hints of the perplexity that was to come two years hence. By insisting that this
Spot contains everything, then discovering that it does not but
energetically redefining it so that it does, Wordsworth expresses
the immensity of the expectations he has placed in It (Dorothy,
Grasmere, *The Recluse*, Nature—the name is unimportant) and
warns of the disaster should it fail to contain them all.

To be 'Home at Grasmere', in the simplest way, is to return
to childish innocence and maternal protection, a 'haunt of pure

affections' where 'I am safe, yes, one at least is safe'. And the return, which once seemed an act of conquest or courage or sacrifice, turns out to be 'smooth, easy, without obstacle'. He appeals to the place to possess him—'Embrace me then, ye Hills, and close me in'—as a beautiful, mild, gay, soft, peaceful guardian and shelter of the night. Folded in its motherly embrace, he feels the most important sensation,

> The one sensation that is here; 'tis here,
> Here as it found its way . . .
> . . . but I cannot name it, 'tis the sense
> Of majesty, and beauty, and repose,
> A blended holiness of earth and sky,
> Something that makes this individual Spot,
> This small Abiding-place of many Men,
> A termination, and a last retreat,
> A Centre, come from wheresoe'er you will,
> A whole without dependence or defect,
> Made for itself; and happy in itself,
> Perfect Contentment, Unity entire.   (137–51)

But he is also a possessor as well as one possessed:

> . . . the unappropriated bliss hath found
> An owner, and that owner I am he.
> The Lord of this enjoyment is on earth
> And in my breast.   (MS. B only.)

Through Dorothy's presence, Home at Grasmere is also a blissful marriage with the present as well as a nostalgic vision of the past, as hand in hand with solitary steps and slow they make their way. With echoes of Milton's paradox of the shared solitude of Adam and Eve after the Fall (as opposed to their shared unity before), Wordsworth predicts for Dorothy and himself a discovery of the paradise within, happier far, that Michael had promised Adam:

> A pair receding from the common world,
> Might in that hallow'd spot to which our steps
> Were tending, in that individual nook,
> Might, even thus early, for ourselves secure.

And in the midst of these unhappy times,
A portion of the blessedness which love
And knowledge, will, we trust, hereafter give
To all the vales of Earth and all mankind.

(MSS. A and B.)

If this is to be a new and better Eden ('. . . among the bowers / Of blissful Eden this [boon] was neither given, / Nor could be given'), Dorothy's presence is essential, for

. . . Where'er my footsteps turned,
Her Voice was like a hidden Bird that sang,
The thought of her was like a flash of light,
Or an *unseen* companionship, a breath,
Or fragrance independent of the wind.   (90–4)

The elaborate comparison between their condition and that of the pair of swans now missing ('they a pair, / And we a solitary pair like them') is anticipated at the beginning of the poem by a metaphor later deleted, in which William and Dorothy are

. . . like Birds
Which by the intruding Fowler had been scar'd,
Two of a scatter'd brood that could not bear
To live in loneliness; 'tis long since we,
Remembering much and hoping more, found means
To walk abreast tho' in a narrow path
With undivided steps.

Yet halfway through the poem, at the end of the passage most insistently celebrating the bliss of their solitude, the beauty of the creatures that surround them, and their invulnerability to circumstance, Wordsworth seems to realize that what he has been praising as the ultimate centre of passivity and invulnerability is death:

. . . the Stream
Is flowing, and will never cease to flow,
And I shall float upon that Stream again.
By such forgetfulness the Soul becomes,
Words cannot say, how beautiful; then hail,
Hail to the visible Presence, hail to thee,

> Delightful Valley, habitation fair!
> And to whatever else of outward form
> Can give us inward help, can purify,
> And elevate, and harmonise, and soothe,
> And steal away, and for a while deceive
> And lap in pleasing rest, and bear us on
> Without desire in full complacency,
> Contemplating perfection absolute
> And entertained as in a placid sleep. (294–308)

As the tone of 'forgetfulness', 'for a while deceive' and 'complacency' seems to become as perplexing for Wordsworth as it does for the reader, the poem suddenly becomes more apologetic, explanatory, and defiant. And the Wordsworth speaking it is a very different person. He insists first that it has not been 'tenderness of mind' that has led them to seek here 'Love, perfect love'. Even here can be heard the awful human voice which may have been made

> The ready Organ of articulate sounds
> From ribaldry, impiety, or wrath
> Issuing when shame hath ceased to check the brawls
> Of some abused Festivity—

And he does not, he says, shrink from such evil reality with disgust. The human qualities that are to be found here, though 'old / Substantial virtues have a firmer tone, / Than in the bare and ordinary world', are not static. They are achieved by activity, and defined by narrative. Life at Grasmere is not after all perpetual noon, because each dawn is a new beginning, bringing 'alternate progress and impediment, and yet a growing prospect in the main'.

Most striking, however, is Wordsworth's redefinition of solitude. To be Home at Grasmere, it now seems, is not to be alone at all, for

> . . . he truly is alone,
> He of the multitude whose eyes are doomed
> To hold a vacant commerce day by day
> With objects wanting life, repelling love;
> He by the vast Metropolis immured,

Where pity shrinks from unremitting calls,
Where numbers overwhelm humanity,
And neighbourhood serves rather to divide
Than to unite.

In contrast, at Grasmere, 'Society is here / A true community'. Their state of life now, it appears, is not placidly contented after all, but full of the hope that there will come no 'dearth of ought / That keeps in health the insatiable mind' and that 'we shall have for knowledge and for love / Abundance'. It is, in fact, a rather tenuous hope, to be realized only if they are worthy of it. Grasmere now is to be earned, not possessed, and to share their struggles and console their disappointments they have (in this spring of 1800) John Wordsworth (A stranger of our Father's house), Sara and Mary Hutchinson (sisters of our hearts), and Coleridge (a brother of our hearts).

Home at Grasmere, then, ceases to be a vision of an ideal past recaptured and a passive reflection of an idealized present and becomes instead the habitation of people who live neither out of the world nor at its centre, and who have worldly anxieties about the future and their isolation from the activities of the more densely inhabited world. Just before the passage that was to become the Prospectus for *The Recluse*, Wordsworth rather harshly turns against the passivity he had praised, calls it hedonistic, and proposes for himself a role from which even Dorothy is explicitly excluded. Announcing that the end of life is not enjoyment, that 'something must be done', that 'ill-advised Ambition' and Pride are real temptations that he must resist, Wordsworth asserts the privacy of his own identity:

Possessions have I that are solely mine,
Something within which yet is shared by none,
Not even the nearest to me and most dear,
Something which power and effort may impart,
I would impart it, I would spread it wide,
Immortal in the world which is to come.

And these possessions, he makes clear, include a propensity for violence, impulsiveness, disobedience. Pleased by tales of conflict 'more than a wise man ought to be',

> ... I wish,
> Fret, burn, and struggle, and in soul am there.

The flames of love, longing, contempt and quest may have been
suppressed by Nature sanctioned by reason, but they will live on
even though their 'office' has been changed. Echoing Othello, he
bids farewell to the more obvious forms of militancy:

> Then farewell to the Warrior's schemes, farewell
> The forwardness of Soul which looks that way
> Upon a less incitement than the cause
> Of Liberty endangered, and farewell
> That other hope, long mine, the hope to fill
> The heroic trumpet with the Muse's breath!

Yet he welcomes the dangers he does attack: the fear and awe and
hell of looking into the mind of man and singing the espousal
verse of the great consummation of the mind and the world. He is
fully aware that he is rejecting a view like that of Saint-Évremond
who like many of his contemporaries insisted that 'the State of a
Solitary Person, is a state of Violence. ... What distinction is
there between Death and Retirement, between Solitude and the
Grave? To live then as Man, 'tis necessary to converse with
Men.'[1] And in rejecting this conclusion, he takes some 850 lines
to try to name what other way is possible for a man who wishes
to reconcile his personal inclinations with his public ambitions
and responsibilities. 'Home at Grasmere' is certainly the only
major attempt before Keats (in the *Fall of Hyperion* as well as the
letters) to confront the disparity between poet, man and dreamer
in literary, social and psychological terms.

The ambiguity of Grasmere, even in 1800, leads finally to an
ambiguity in Wordsworth's attitude toward his role as poet, as
son and brother, as a moral man living 'far from the living and
dead wilderness / Of the thronged World' who wishes both to
escape from it and forcibly to harmonize its jarring. Though most
of Wordsworth's ambition to do for the world some good by
fulfilling the obligation he saw conferred upon him because of his
'possessions' seems to have been directed toward the slowly

---

[1] *Works* (London, 1700), I, 311–12, as quoted by Herbert Davis, *Jonathan
Swift: Essays on his Satire and Other Studies* (New York, 1964), p. 262.

progressing *Recluse,* when the second edition of *Lyrical Ballads* was published in January 1801, Wordsworth and his circle at first were confident that a career had been established, that the poet could now speak with the authority of an important national literary figure. In his letter to C. J. Fox accompanying a presentation copy of this edition Wordsworth announced rather pompously his assumption of the role of defender of the 'blessings of independent domestic life'. His brother John, in London waiting to assume command of the *Earl of Abergavenny,* was given the job of delivering the presentation letters to Longman and collecting the first London reactions, paying particular attention to the effect of the test poems: 'Michael', 'The Brothers', John's favourite 'Joanna', and 'Nutting'. The four poems of course were new to this edition, and in three of them Wordsworth boldly asserted his strength and his difference. In 'Michael' (and to a lesser extent in 'The Brothers'), James Smith has argued, Wordsworth allowed himself to contemplate suffering unadulterated in any way—'as, for example, with the satisfaction of playing either to himself or to an audience'—and concluded that the extinction of suffering was the extinction of life.[1] And publishing 'Nutting' must have been Wordsworth's way of testing in public what he had been composing for *The Prelude.* Like the Spots of Time and their analogues, this poem indulges a full expression of delight in the vulnerability of a secluded natural scene, and that delight is exceeded only by the joy produced by violently destroying it. Significance and guilt, as so often in key passages of *The Prelude,* are almost synonymous, though the language there is rarely so explicitly sexual. The three poems almost make clear the way in which the ambitions announced in 'Home at Grasmere' could have found literary form, for here indeed Wordsworth makes an enormous effort to discover in experience remote from public life feelings and meanings absolutely central to all forms of human life wherever it is lived intensely.

But Wordsworth and his family could not sustain for long their confident expectations. No review could possibly have matched Wordsworth's hopes, and the amused collecting of

[1] 'Wordsworth: A Preliminary Survey', *Scrutiny,* VII (1938–39), 33–55.

opinions did not last long. There must have been desperation as well as exasperation in Wordsworth's reply to Charles Lamb's tactless admission that all the best poems had already appeared in the first edition. On February 15th Lamb complained to Thomas Manning that his honesty had earned him 'four sweating pages from my Reluctant Letter-Writer' who ' "was compelled to wish that my range of sensibility was more extended" ', and added that he had received an equally long ('equally sweaty and more tedious') chastisement from Coleridge.

More pathetic, however, is Wordsworth's exchange with a Miss Taylor, who with her brother John (one time editor of the *Sun*), had thanked Wordsworth for a presentation copy and, apparently, inquired politely about his biography and circumstances. Wordsworth's reply, on April 9th, must have told Miss Taylor far more than she could have wished to know. After an autobiographical statement and a recommendation that she read *Descriptive Sketches* and *An Evening Walk* (although 'juvenile', 'inflated', 'obscure', they contain 'many new images, and vigorous lines'), he supplied Miss Taylor with more than thirty lines of corrections and revisions wherein she 'will perceive in what manner I have attempted gradually to purify my diction'. The public poet, having failed to become the acknowledged national poet, seems to have tried any device to cling to readers who appeared to take him at his own estimate. In the same week that Wordsworth answered Miss Taylor and her brother with equally detailed letters, his brother John, writing to Mary Hutchinson, complains of the world's mistreatment of both Wordsworth and Coleridge:

Indeed it is a most melancholy thing to think that either of them should want a reasonable share of money, considering the times—that William's health should be hurt by anxiety which I fear it is—that C. should be obliged to write for newspapers.[1]

In spite of the hopes announced in 'Home at Grasmere', Grasmere apparently could not be the eccentric source of a central voice after all; it could not be 'a whole without dependence

---

[1] Quotations here and subsequently from the letters of John Wordsworth are taken from the manuscripts in the Wordsworth Library in Grasmere.

or defect . . . unity entire' nor could it offer a congenial environment for this sort of composition. Having relinquished his ambition to change the world by acting in it, Wordsworth must now have realized that speaking to an uncaring world was likely to be even less effectual. Unquestionably Grasmere had fulfilled all his nostalgic visions. His and Dorothy's later accounts of these years attest to their happiness, as does Coleridge's sustained envy of it. But the aggressive ambitions that were somehow to be controlled and directed from this peaceful source had been blunted and deflected. It is pointless to be an oracle on a mountain top if the rest of humanity is out of the range of your voice, and no one comes to consult you.

Whether the cause of the anxiety John mentions was the disappointment William felt at the reception of the second edition of *Lyrical Ballads,* or was more simply financial, it is true that the rest of 1801 was indeed for Wordsworth what the Chronological Table of Hutchinson's Oxford edition succinctly calls an 'unproductive interval'. Although Dorothy told John in late March that William was going on with *The Recluse,* and in April John received two sheets of alterations for *The Prelude* and other poems that Sara Hutchinson had copied out while she was at Grasmere in March, Wordsworth wrote almost no new poems during the year except 'Louisa', 'I travelled among unknown men', and 'To a Lady who . . .'.

(ii)

Perhaps it is misleading to suggest that Wordsworth's disillusion as a public poet encouraged him to narrow his attention from the world to Dorothy and to confirm the dependence on her that had begun at Goslar. 'Home at Grasmere' in fact suggests that these were not alternative modes of life but components of the same ambition. A poet's inactive year, inevitably, is a year about which little is known, and only deductions based on what followed it offer any insight. The few poems that can confidently be assigned to 1801 and the first months of 1802 seem entirely lacking in the intensity of personal investment that finds a place

even in such simple later poems as the two addressed to a butterfly. 'I travelled among unknown men', for instance, is explicitly
an autobiographical love poem, but its tone is so far from being
insistent that Wordsworth used it on separate occasions to declare
his love both for Mary and for Dorothy. A fully articulated
attempt to create in words a new sort of poet in a new sort of
Grasmere did not really take shape for a year, and then only
after (and along with) a painstaking reconsideration of what he
had been doing until 1801.

To be sure, Wordsworth's time and attention in 1801 were
occupied by activities only indirectly related to his unrealized
ambition as a public poet, but just as likely to suspend his literary
activities. The demands that a suffering Coleridge made on
William and Dorothy during the first half of the year must have
been exhausting to their energy and sympathy. For every one of
his projects, whether setting up a chemistry laboratory or emi-
grating to the Azores, Coleridge demanded his friends' co-
operation. And Hartley Coleridge, then four-and-a-half and
sickly, spent a good deal of time at Town End while he attended
school in Grasmere.

The disadvantages of living that close to Coleridge included
more than demands on Wordsworth's time. Misunderstandings
flourished. When Coleridge, ignoring the cautions of John
Wordsworth, persisted in his plan to move to St. Michaels in the
Azores, he imagined an arrangement with a bookseller (one had
not yet been consulted) whereby his future writing would be
mortgaged against a loan of £40, with someone acting as security
'in the case that Death or Disease should occasion a non-perform-
ance of my Engagement' (to Poole, 5 July 1801). Wordsworth,
perhaps tactlessly, intervened in what he saw as an attempt to
make Thomas Poole the guarantor of this arrangement. Writing
to Poole in July, Wordsworth warned him that Coleridge's
estimates of his need were far too low, and condemned the
mortgage arrangement (by this time to involve a loan of £100)
as unsound for both Coleridge and the bookseller. Instead, Wordsworth suggested, Poole ought to give Coleridge £50 as an out-
right loan, 'unshackled by any conditions'. However reasonable

and admirable Wordsworth's intentions, he seems to have offended both Poole and Coleridge, so that 'Error generates Error': Poole wrote to Coleridge in replying to Wordsworth's letter, thus revealing Wordsworth's doubts, then Poole on his own initiative applied to the Wedgwoods for the money, thus disturbing the delicate balance of Coleridge's relations with his benefactors, and finally Poole offended Coleridge by suggesting that Coleridge borrow the money from his parents. Only a Coleridge could have constructed from a single tactless letter such a maze of resentments and distresses, but perhaps only a Wordsworth would have allowed himself so to suffer from it.

But on other occasions that year Wordsworth was as quick to take offence as Coleridge. After William and Dorothy's earlier estrangement from the unstable Charles Lloyd at Alfoxden, a friendship between Lloyd and the Wordsworths seems to have grown up again—perhaps through the mediation of the Clarksons and by virtue of Christopher Wordsworth's long engagement to Charles' sister Priscilla—when Lloyd and his family moved to Ambleside. But by April something so unpleasant had happened that John Wordsworth, replying to Dorothy's accounts of it, calls Lloyd 'an incomprehensible Knave and ass' to deceive his father. Perhaps Lloyd's association with the opinions of Lamb and Manning about *Lyrical Ballads* became known, and offended the Wordsworths' family loyalties. Although Lloyd had chastised Manning for underrating the poems, he grants 'their total nakedness in point of imagination—their puerile minuteness—their cold accuracy' and agrees with Manning that 'it is a perversion of the human mind to cultivate a love for [inanimate nature] as a primary object'.[1] Whatever the cause—it may also have been some injustice to Christopher—the Wordsworths kept away as much as possible from the Lloyds. Although they encountered one another rather frequently and at times with some amicability for the rest of the year, by June of 1802 Dorothy writes to the Hutchinsons that 'we are determined to cut them entirely as far as Will goes; there is one chain about us, Priscilla [though she had

[1] Charles Lloyd to Thomas Manning, 31 March 1801; in *The Lloyd-Manning Letters*, edited by F. L. Beaty (Bloomington, Indiana, 1957).

not yet married Christopher], but she shall only drag us to Brathay about once a year'.

Ill health as well contributed to Wordsworth's poetic inactivity in 1801, but lacking Dorothy's *Journal* for the first nine months of the year it is difficult to tell how much of a hindrance it was. In February he declined Francis Wrangham's invitation to Yorkshire on the grounds that he was too poor to ride and too weak to walk there, and in May Dorothy says she was obliged to put away all his manuscripts. Yet in September Wordsworth accompanied Sir William Rush and his family to Glasgow for the wedding of Laura Rush and Basil Montagu.

The absence of Dorothy's day-to-day record for most of 1801, as well as the lack of poems, makes Grasmere in 1801 seem more an ordinary village than part of a career. Visits of friendship to the Clarksons, of compassion to Keswick, are the sort of activities anyone might undertake at any time. And the existing letters give no indication of any extraordinary activity, social or intellectual, in the household until autumn. During this year there must have been plenty of time for reading, and the prolific activity of the following year makes it reasonable to assume that 1801, like the year at Goslar, was for Wordsworth a year of sustained self-education. In his letter to Wrangham in February, however, Wordsworth shows some of the limitations of Grasmere as a centre for study: 'We live quite out of the way of new books; I have not seen a single one since I came here, now 13 months ago.' So the box of books and clothes sent from London in January of 1802 was the occasion of considerable excitement. The evening it arrived Dorothy sat by William's bedside and 'read in [Campbell's] *The Pleasures of Hope* to him, which came in the box', a poem Wordsworth had been looking forward to seeing for a year. Although Dorothy's *Journal* after February 1st, when the box arrived, indicates the considerable variety it contained, their reading between October and February, and presumably earlier, seems to have been largely confined to a few of the volumes of Anderson's *British Poets*.

Because this immense anthology played so large a part in Wordsworth's education—and Coleridge's—it deserves some description. Published in London and Edinburgh in 1792–5, edited by an Edinburgh physician named Robert Anderson, priced at £8, it consists of thirteen royal octavo volumes, printed in double columns, containing extensive selections from well over a hundred major and minor English poets from Chaucer, Wyatt and Surrey (vol. I) to Logan, Warton, Cotton and Blacklock (vol. XI). Volumes XII and XIII consist of translations of the classics, including Pope's *Iliad* and *Odyssey*, Dryden's Virgil, Cruch's Lucretius. Each poet is given a generous biographical and critical introduction consisting of a précis by Anderson of earlier biographies, or for more contemporary poets a biography of Anderson's own composition. For all its lapses in taste and text, the edition represents a rather magnificent library of English verse, and it is not surprising that Wordsworth, when he met Anderson in 1814, should have expressed to him his indebtedness. In these volumes, he told Anderson, he first discovered Drayton, Daniel and the minor Elizabethans. So indispensable was the collection that Coleridge owned at least two sets in his lifetime, both heavily annotated, and the Wordsworths seem to have had one in addition to the one John left behind at Grasmere in September 1800. John wrote to Dorothy in May 1801, just before sailing for the first time in command of the *Earl of Abergavenny*, that he had Anderson's *British Poets* with him, and would be grateful if William would point out particular poems 'in Poets such as Logan for instance'. Yet Dorothy and Mary that December are both reading Robert Bruce, who appears with Logan in volume XI. And even though William must have been using Anderson's text for the Chaucer he was translating in 1801–2, neither copy preserved at Dove Cottage shows any signs of hard use of volume I.

So even if the greatest part of the working library Wordsworth had with him at Grasmere in 1801 was restricted to Anderson's *Poets*, he was well supplied. Here on one November evening he and Dorothy were reading Chaucer and Bishop Hall (vols. I and II) while Mary read Thomson (vol. IX). Ten days later Mary read out 'a poem by Daniel upon Learning' ('Musophilus', vol. IV), three weeks later the first canto of the *Faery Queen* (vol. II), and in

January Dorothy read (perhaps from vol. v) the first book of
Paradise Lost. Even after the box of new books arrived in January
1802, Anderson's popularity continued: book IX of *Paradise Lost*
on February 2nd, Smollett's life (vol. x) on February 4th, the life
and poems of Ben Jonson (vol. IV), Shakespeare's *The Lover's
Complaint* (vol II) on May 5th. Though Anderson must have been
almost as central in Wordsworth's reading during 1801 as Percy's
Reliques and Bertram's *Travels* had been during the winter in
Goslar, the very extent and diversity of the anthology makes its
importance to Wordsworth's education impossible to assess very
specifically. But during the year he *could* have read with considerable thoroughness the work and life of any significant poet from
the time of Chaucer to the end of the eighteenth century, with a
few exceptions (Traherne, for instance). Of course the extent of
Wordsworth's reading in Anderson, and elsewhere, is far easier
to locate after Dorothy's *Journal* is resumed in October 1801, and
the influence of William's reading is obviously more clearly
appreciable after he had begun to write again.

Because Dorothy's *Journals* do survive from October 1801 (the
entries for the first few days are casual enough to suggest that
volumes now lost covered previous months), it is possible to be
more orderly about the end of Wordsworth's 'unproductive
interval' than about its beginning, and more direct about Wordsworth's sense of what it now meant to be a poet in Grasmere.
Perhaps significantly, the resumption of a day-to-day record
almost coincides with a reunion of Wordsworth and Coleridge.
Sometime late in September 1801 (Montagu's wedding was on
the 6th but Wordsworth was still in Scotland on the 22nd),
Wordsworth returned to Grasmere to be host to a healthier but
even more distressed Coleridge, who had gone to Yorkshire in
July and returned just about the time William went to Scotland.
Coleridge told William Godwin on the 22nd that he had given up
the Azores and now suffers intensely from recent 'additional
sources of Disquietude' which he will not relate to Godwin because
they have not known one another long enough. But Coleridge's
reticence does not outlive the second paragraph, where he makes
it quite clear (though he is far more candid in his letter to Southey

a month later) that the disquietude is domestic and that flight, now to London rather than the Azores, is an escape from Sara Coleridge rather than the damp North.

Coleridge's presence at Town End at the beginning of October has been demonstrated by Mrs. Moorman's discovery of Coleridge's 'Ode to the Rain' written in the Wordsworths' commonplace book and called there 'Lines written by Coleridge in bed at Grasmere on Thursday night October 1st or rather on the morning of Friday October 2nd 1801'[1]. The poet's complaint therefore is not directed at someone visiting him but rather at a simultaneous visitor at Dove Cottage (perhaps Clarkson or Wilkinson, either of whom may have been in Coleridge's eyes 'not very pleasant' though in everyone else's 'very worthy'). The speaker's pretence of being in his own house is a reasonable enough fiction, and the rest of the details of the poem fit clearly the situation of October 1801: Wordsworth, 'a dear old Friend e'en now is here . . . after long absence now first met'. William would have just returned from his month in Scotland, and since Coleridge was at Gallow Hill, Durham, Bishop Middleham and Dunsdale at least until August 19th, the poets can have met but briefly, if at all, since July.

The impression of extraordinary sociability at Town End that Dorothy's record of visitors gives may be misleading, a result simply of there being no similar record for the previous months. But suddenly the cottage does seem to contain a great variety of people, so that Coleridge might well say ' We three dear friends! in truth, we groan / Impatiently to be alone'. Coleridge, back at Keswick on October 5th, may have used Mrs. Southey's presence at Greta Hall with her sister as an excuse for still another overnight visit to Grasmere, for Dorothy's *Journal* opens with the entry for October 10th: 'Coleridge went to Keswick, after we had built Sara's seat.' And his visits continued to be frequent and relatively long throughout the autumn. He was at Grasmere again from October 15th to 19th, then home at Greta Hall on October 23rd to meet Mary Hutchinson when she arrived there

[1] 'Wordsworth's Commonplace Book,' *Notes and Queries*, 202 (September 1957).

on her way to Grasmere, was back in Grasmere from the 6th to the 9th of November when the Wordsworths and Mary accompanied him back to Keswick and there parted from him, for he was on his way to London (and later Nether Stowey) for an absence that was to last for more than sixteen weeks. But even with the help of the *Journal*, it is difficult to tell just what the order of visitors at Town End in October and early November was. Tom Hutchinson arrived there on October 16th, accompanied the Wordsworths on an excursion to Penny Bridge and Coniston, and was still there on the 25th. The Clarksons arrived on the 28th and stayed until November 5th. Mary Hutchinson presumably arrived in Grasmere from Keswick shortly after they left, apparently during the days between November 5th and 9th for which the *Journal* entries have been torn out (though it is possible that she had come over from Keswick on the day she was expected, October 25th). Mary's visit lasted until December 28th, when the Wordsworths themselves went to spend a month with the Clarksons at Eusemere. In any case, there can have been little time, or even space, for much literary activity at Town End during part of this period, and there is no reference to William reading, let alone writing, until mid-November, after Coleridge left for London.

But in November, with Mary settled at Town End until the end of the year, Wordsworth had ideal circumstances in which to begin work: two admiring listeners and eager secretaries, and no danger of interruption from Keswick. At the beginning, the intellectual activity of the household seems to have been primarily recreational: sitting by the fire on November 15th to read Bishop Hall and Chaucer (William and Dorothy), and Thomson (Mary). The next day William is reading Spenser, as he is on November 24th, the day Mary read Daniel's 'Musophilus' to them. But on December 2nd, almost two months after the *Journal* has resumed, Dorothy for the first time mentions William writing: a translation ('attempted' is her verb) of 'The Manciple's Tale'. Within four days, William has finished as well a translation of 'The Cuckow and the Nightingale', while the nightly reading of Chaucer continued.

Translating, which Wordsworth did rarely considering his command of French and German as well as Latin, must have been an exercise that again was as much recreational as imaginative. That Wordsworth worked so hard on tales he must have found uncongenial is a tribute to his perseverance, for he had to reconcile his loyalty to Chaucer's language and an obedience to English verse forms with his manifest displeasure with the subjects. 'The Manciple's Tale' is an especially unlikely place to have begun unless these were indeed recreational or therapeutic problems he set himself: the couplets must have been trying, and the story itself, bringing together the fabliau and the beast fable, seems an unlikely story for Wordsworth to have wanted to tell himself, even through the remoteness of translation. Phoebus' talking crow, witnessing the infidelity of Phoebus' wife, reports what he has seen to his master, who kills the wife, resolves to kill himself, and casts the white crow, tongueless and featherless and now black, 'unto perdition'. And the cynical moral drawn by the manciple is concerned not with chastity but with gossip. Though he revised the translation for publication in 1840, Wordsworth finally withdrew it, apparently at the urging of Quillinan and Miss Fenwick. But to his daughter Dora Quillinan, he defended the morality of the tale in terms that suggest he understood it less well than they did: 'How could the mischief of telling truth, merely because it *is* truth, be more feelingly exemplified? . . . How vividly is impressed the mischief of jealous vigilance, and how truly and touchingly in contrast with the world's judgements are the transgressions of a woman in a low rank of life and one in high estate placed on the same level, treated.' The humourless moralizing of his letter is echoed as well by many of the revisions in his manuscript, most of them presumably made when he was revising it in 1840. Throughout his 'modernizations' Wordsworth seems to have tried to be as literal as possible ('. . . no further deviation from the original has been made than was necessary for the fluent reading and instant understanding of the Author'), and the opening lines of 'The Manciple's Tale', in their two versions, show how he went about it. Faced with this couplet—

> When Phoebus dwelled here in this earth adoun
> As olde bookes maken mencioun—

Wordsworth's first step is to get rid of the awkwardly emphatic 'adoun' by simply reversing the verb and the adverb:

> When Phoebus here below on earth did dwell—
> As ancient histories to us do tell.   (MS. 1)

But then, perhaps because the lines now have more prepositions and adverbs than sense requires, he at some point altered the sense to give it some tone at least, though it sounds rather epic for the manciple:

> When Phoebus took delight on earth to dwell
> Among mankind, as ancient stories tell.

Wordsworth's misgivings about the sexual explicitness of the crow's tale account for the most drastic departures from the original, though the most elaborate of these were probably made in 1840. Either immediately, or during the course of forty years, the line first translated as 'They took their fill of love and lover's rage' ('Anon they wroghten all hir lust volage') became 'To love's delights themselves they did engage' and finally ended as 'In their loose dalliance they anon engage'. And Chaucer's verb 'swyve', apparently from the beginning all too transitive for Wordsworth, was replaced with a moralistic, almost legalistic, noun: 'For on thy bed thy wyf I saugh hym swyve' becomes '[I] saw him in guilty converse with thy wife'.

When Wordsworth two days later moved on to 'The Prioress' Tale' he may have found the matter more congenial but he certainly found a verse form considerably more challenging. The couplets of 'The Manciple's Tale' formed a two-line unity within which syntactical rearrangements caused little trouble with the rhymes. But the rhyme royal of 'The Prioress' Tale' (ababbcc) presented a task that Wordsworth could not always fulfil successfully: in one stanza (IX) he simply added a line (ababcddc), in others (XIX and XXXIV) he altered the rhyme royal pattern (ababcdc, abacddc). In working on this tale, and in translating 'Troilus and Cressida', Wordsworth for the first time attempted

rhyme royal, and initiated a series of technical experiments even
more extensive than those he had undertaken in the spring of
1798 when he was composing 'Peter Bell'. Rhyme royal of
course was to appear again and more significantly in 'Resolution
and Independence'. In most of the poems written after this brief
attempt at modernizing Chaucer, Wordsworth made deliberate
use of the stanzaic form of his poems, regarding the complexities
of rhyme as a challenge to the poet's imagination, not simply to
his technical facility at imitating traditional ballad forms. Certainly
in effect if not intention, the translations from Chaucer were
first exercises in the particular poetic techniques Wordsworth
more fully and interestingly explored in the great poems of the
spring of 1802. His translation of 'The Cuckow and the Nightingale,' a poem still attributed to Chaucer in the early nineteenth
century, was even more important as a specific step toward the
theme and language of 'Resolution and Independence'.[1]

Yet however seriously he undertook it, the writing that Wordsworth did during the quieter weeks of early December as he and
Dorothy and Mary sat around the fire could hardly be called
original composition. None of them seems to have assumed that
the modernizations were significant poetic statements or indeed
that they were intended for publication. Rather they seem, in
Dorothy's *Journal*, to be domestic activities, like the nightly readings and almost daily walks.

(iii)

At some time late in 1801 or very early in 1802, Wordsworth
must have made clear, if not public, his intention to marry Mary
Hutchinson. It may well be true, as Bateson suggests,[2] that the
decision was made, or at least contemplated as desirable, when the
Wordsworths spent seven months with Mary at Sockburn on
Tees in the later half of 1799, on their return from Germany.

---

[1] Metrical connections between the Chaucer translations and 'The Leechgatherer' are also pointed out by A. E. M. Conran, 'A Study of Wordsworth's
Resolution and Independence', *PMLA*, LXXV (1960), 66–74.
[2] *Wordsworth: A Reinterpretation* (London, 1954, rev. edn. 1956), p. 156.

But John Wordsworth, whose close friendship with Mary began during the six weeks they were visitors to Grasmere together in the winter of 1799–1800, was still writing to her in the tone of an undeclared lover rather than a prospective brother-in-law in May 1801. His letter to her in September 1802 in which he either wistfully or humorously gives her up to his brother seems prompted by surprise and regret. The earliest hint of the betrothal is Dorothy's reference to Molly Fisher teasing Mary in November 1801, unless Coleridge is slyly alluding to it in his verse letter to Isabella Addison and Joanna Hutchinson in August 1801. The intimacy of the Wordsworths, the Coleridges and the Hutchinsons, and their isolation from the rest of the social, public world is nowhere more clearly indicated than in the matter of William and Mary's engagement. Though Coleridge writing to his wife in February 1802 refers to the wedding plans as an acknowledged fact, Dorothy merely says to her brother Richard in late February 1802 that 'one of the Miss Hutchinsons has spent seven weeks of the winter with us', and first tells him in June of the impending marriage.

In deciding to marry, and to choose Mary Hutchinson (Bateson is persuasive in regarding them as separate decisions), Wordsworth obviously was not precipitous nor acting with complete independence. Mary, calmly admired by Coleridge, rather more warmly loved by John Wordsworth, a confidante and childhood friend of Dorothy's, seems to have been the creation of those who could make of her ordinariness the sort of vividly satisfying figure they wished. It is entirely appropriate that William should see her as part of a household, and that his only poem directly about the marriage—written a month after he and Dorothy had spent an April morning in the garden at Town End reading Spenser's *Prothalamion*—should address not Mary but the cottage. Mary is

> A gentle Maid, whose heart is lowly bred,
> Whose pleasures are in wild fields gather'd

and she, coming to the house and its 'little Nook of mountain ground'

Will come to you [i.e. Town End]; to you herself will wed
And love the blessed life that we lead here.

The wedding will take place after William and Dorothy

Two burning months let summer overleap,
And, coming back with Her who will be ours,
Into thy bosom we again shall creep.

By the time these lines were written, of course, Wordsworth
had begun to resolve more than the question of Mary's place at
Grasmere, and a great deal of writing had intervened between
Mary's departure from Grasmere at the end of December 1801
and the composition of this poem in May 1802. When she left,
and when William and Dorothy resumed their correspondence
with Annette Vallon, William had written nothing that winter
except the Chaucer translations. The idyllic career projected in
'Home at Grasmere' was still unrealized, and apparently Wordsworth had not replaced it with any new definition of a position
within which he might live and from which he might speak.
Almost exclusive intimacy with Dorothy had been an essential
part of the 'Home at Grasmere' vision, but during the year,
everything suggests, visionary intimacy had given way to a
sort of domestic coziness—unremarkable, unproductive, and
perhaps discouragingly boring. To bring Mary into that atmosphere could mean, for William, a means of prolonging its
longueurs indefinitely; or given Dorothy's feelings, it could be a
way of disrupting the mood sufficiently to provoke William to a
new decision about what he was to become.

However formidable Wordsworth's sense of responsibility to
Annette and Caroline, however necessary he felt his trip to
France in September, more than one passage in Dorothy's *Journal*
suggests that the part the journey played in causing the difficulty
of setting a date for the wedding may have begun in Dorothy's
possessive attitude toward her brother. It may in fact have been at
Dorothy's insistence that they went to France at all: on 22 March
1802 she writes: 'We talked a good deal about C[oleridge] and
other interesting things. We resolved to see Annette, and that

Wm. should go to Mary.' The words hardly suggest the deter-
minations of a man bent on making amends, but they could well
be the words Dorothy might have chosen to describe her fight
against time for her brother.

The intensity of her attachment to William may have been as
distressing to Dorothy as it was to the Reverend Knight when he
first published the *Journals* without mentioning his relentless
exclusion of every one of those passages, now restored, that allude
in any way to the strength of her feelings for her brother, her
yearning depression in his absence, her pleasure in caring for him,
kissing him, comforting and caressing him. And the possibility of
this feeling being incestuous unquestionably occurred to Dorothy.
The only novel she ever mentions reading (in her *Journal* for 5
February 1802) is an anonymous three-volume epistolary romance
published in 1791 and called *Wanley Penson, The Story of a
Melancholy Man*. On that 'cold snowy morning' says Dorothy, 'I
read the story of Isabel in Wanley Penson'.[1] The story of Isabel
and Wanley, the central narrative of the book, is a conventionally
complicated *Sturm und Drang* tale, beginning with the loss of
Wanley's fiancée, his despair of ever loving again, his wish for a
sister to comfort him, his rescue and falling in love with a gypsy
girl who is later revealed to be his lost sister Isabel, and finally
Isabel's departure from Wanley because 'as she *dared* to love me
only as a sister, she resolved not to love me at all'. There is much
in the novel that may have comforted Dorothy, for the innocent
Wanley sentimentally idealizes the love of a brother for a sister as
the highest possible kind: 'Indeed I know of no affection so tender,
and so abstracted from every sort of gross idea, as that between a
loving brother and sister' because 'the love of a brother for a sister
unites in it all the tenderness which her sex inspires, with the
most perfect purity'. But his idealization is rendered naive, in a

[1] Both the de Selincourt two-volume (1941) edition of the *Journals* and Miss
Darbishire's more accurate World's Classics edition (1958) give the following
sentence in the entry for 5 February 1802: 'I read the story of [?] in [?].' On closer
scrutiny in the manuscript version, however, the words clearly appear as 'Isabel'
and 'Wanley'. Among the books in Wordsworth's library at his death was a three-
volume novel called *Wanley Penson, The Story of a Melancholy Man*, published
anonymously (attributed conjecturally to 'Sadler of Chippenham') in 1791.

way that must have distressed Dorothy, by Isabel's more sophisticated account of her own nature. Though she feels that she has changed her love for Wanley from carnal to spiritual, she nevertheless repents her 'crime' in having once thought of him as a lover and insists that she can never live with him because even if they avoided 'actual sin' they would be 'tampering with evil'. Wanley, still uncomprehending, laments that he has been the unwitting cause of such a painful passion.

It would be ridiculous to suppose that this rambling, rather incompetent romance could be taken by any reader as a serious dramatization of a relationship between adults. But the fact that Dorothy did read it, probably re-read it (to isolate the 'story of Isabel' from the tangled narrative she would have had to) does demonstrate that she has read an explicit and detailed (if morally and psychologically absurd) discussion of the dangers of precisely the sort of household she had shared with William for the last four years, and that she still hoped to go on sharing. Dorothy had available to her, indeed thrust before her attention, at least one way of seeing her life with William as a sexual temptation, and she can hardly have failed to connect the story in some way with herself, if only to scoff at the parallel.

The December evenings around the fire at Grasmere were not as placid perhaps as they at first seem. Amid quiet reading and careful translating there must have been serious discussions about the future to which Dorothy does not refer; and the three must have been very much aware of how drastically their relations with one another, if not the outward patterns of their lives, would change within a year. At some time late in 1801, thanks to the negotiations that led to the Peace of Amiens, correspondence with Annette Vallon again became possible. The first letter from France arrived at Grasmere on December 21st, brought from Ambleside in fact by Mary. Although it is impossible to know whether it was a letter from Annette written on her own initiative, or her answer to an earlier letter from William, or was a letter from someone in France about Annette, its arrival was not a shock, was even less distressing to the Grasmere household, according to Dorothy, than Coleridge's melancholy report of illness in his bowels. But a new voice had been added, from a distance, to the discussions at Town End.

(iv)

The letter from France arrived on the very day that William, for the first time in at least three months, probably longer, returned to original composition. In the next few days he brought together for reconsideration three poems that he had apparently left untouched since the previous spring, and that had been in process for several years before that: 'The Ruined Cottage' (not yet called 'The Pedlar'), *The Prelude* (called simply 'the poem to Coleridge'), and 'Peter Bell'. All three at the time were rather shapeless works, obviously autobiographical in significance if not in subject, that Wordsworth could complete only when he had decided what sort of poems he wanted to make of them. To finish them now, when so much had happened since their inception, was a task of self-definition. The first large project, which would occupy Wordsworth's literary attention for the next two months, was the re-writing of 'The Ruined Cottage', the story about the sufferings of Margaret later incorporated in book I of *The Excursion*, that Wordsworth at this time thought of as an independent poem of about a thousand lines. But before this work got fully under way, Wordsworth turned for about three days (possibly longer since it is difficult to tell if the lines Mary wrote out for him on December 27th are from book III of *The Prelude* or Part III of 'The Ruined Cottage') to his 'Poem to Coleridge', which had been laid aside months before. Wordsworth had written an almost complete version of 'The Ruined Cottage' at Alfoxden in the winter of 1797–8, 'Peter Bell' was begun in April 1798 ('Tintern Abbey' followed in July), and work on what was to become the first book of *The Prelude* began shortly after William and Dorothy arrived at Goslar in the autumn of 1798. 'Tintern Abbey', finished and published in 1798, presumably had been separated from its maker, but Wordsworth was still preoccupied with the questions it shared with the other three fragmentary compositions whose value he doubted yet. If anything can, these three unfinished long poems and 'Tintern

Abbey' may indicate the direction that Wordsworth's explorations had taken since he left Alfoxden.

'Peter Bell', of course, differs from the other unfinished poems (and from 'Tintern Abbey') in the detachment the narrator takes from his tale. Though the Prologue presents an argument, like that of the Preface to *Lyrical Ballads*, in favour of the mundane imagination, and the narrator repeatedly refers to his assumed audience—their interruptions, their impatience, their boredom— the story is a tale, not an experience, its palpable design is first of all directed at the reader's attention and interest rather than his character; and finally the narrator himself has already come to terms with the story, so that he is not himself being changed as he tells it. The voice is that of a singer rather than a maker, its tone is expressive rather than introspective. As in many of the introspective moments of the early books of *The Prelude*, the initial crime discussed in 'Peter Bell' is one against Nature rather than Man (the beating of the ass), but Nature's voice which (like the Word sent by the potent spirits of the opening of Part III) focuses, exposes, releases Peter's sense of guilt, speaks in humanitarian terms. When Peter hears Rachel sigh that 'Poor thing, 'tis fatherless!'

> ... now does Peter deeply feel
> The heart of Man's a holy thing;
> And Nature, through a world of death,
> Breathes into him a second breath,
> Just like the breath of spring. (text *c.* 1800)

Thus Peter's guilt, no longer metaphysical, becomes social and human, and its reforming influence produces benevolence toward man rather than nature's creatures. 'Peter Bell' was begun as a complement, perhaps even a reply, to the *Ancient Mariner* less than a month after Coleridge brought his finished ballad to Alfoxden. Yet to preserve this tone of detachment in 'Peter Bell' gave Wordsworth an inordinate amount of difficulty. Like *The Prelude* and 'The Pedlar', it was one of the unfinished poems Wordsworth energetically returned to when he undertook revision in the winter of 1801-2.

4

However, the worrying concerns permeating *The Prelude*, 'The Ruined Cottage' and 'Tintern Abbey' are, put most simply, attempts at self-definition rather than moral transformation. These poems do appear to have engaged Wordsworth most fully just at moments when he felt he must give some account of himself to the world, to his friends and relations, or to himself. 'Tintern Abbey', placed so conclusively at the end of *Lyrical Ballads*, seems designed to answer that reader who asks, justifiably, what consciousness operates behind the voice singing in most of these ballads, and why he should attend to it. And the poem was composed just after the Wordsworths had left Alfoxden, to mark time between the expiration of their lease there and their departure with Coleridge for Germany on an excursion the motives for which are still obscure to biographers and probably were to William and Dorothy at the time.

The work done in 1798 and 1799 on 'The Ruined Cottage' and on *The Prelude* was of course more explicitly concerned with self-definition. The 'poem on his own life' begun at Goslar that winter was from its inception an 'appendix' to *The Recluse*, and the composition of its first and second books served Wordsworth as a stabilizing act of autobiography during the winter misery of their isolation in Saxony. Both poems, and 'Tintern Abbey', are moral poems in Arnold's sense of being directed to the question, How to live; in all of them Wordsworth merges autobiographical narrative and philosophical reflection into what will appear to be a final statement about the present quality of the poet's life and the nature of his sensibility; and in all three poems he traces in similar terms and images the loss of a past innocence with its immediacy of experience, and offers a justification for an occupation pursued nevertheless in the faith of a compensating awareness.

Even without the knowledge that line after line describing the Pedlar in early drafts of 'The Ruined Cottage' was later adapted to Wordsworth's first-person account of his own education in *The Prelude*, a reader inevitably sees that the narrator of 'The Ruined Cottage' knows far more about his interlocutor than he ought to, more indeed than any man can know of another, and much more than any reader need know in order to follow the story of Margaret.[1] Like the narrator of 'Tintern Abbey' and of *The Prelude*, the Pedlar as first conceived is a man who has been educated by forms of communion 'not from terror free' with Nature, whose passive sensibility has been acted on in such a way that he has perceived the 'presence and power of greatness' and 'deep feelings' have impressed themselves on his mind. In a manner unnecessary for the narrator of Margaret's story but so essential for the creator of the poem that contains him, the Pedlar's childhood sensibility has been extended and sustained by the repetition of great sights, events, moments, so that he has acquired as well an active power to 'fasten images upon his brain', to compare and judge and discriminate with informed feelings and a moving intellect. But even as a child he could see evidence of a mighty flowing mind in the fixed lineaments of the world he looked upon.

By ascribing all this and more to the Pedlar rather than to himself, Wordsworth apparently felt no need to justify it, and no reason not to elevate and praise the quality of a life that was his own disguised. In his notes to *The Excursion*, written long after this pedlar had been redescribed to match Sara Hutchinson's recollections of James Patrick, Wordsworth was quite candid about identifying himself with the Pedlar:

. . . had I been born in a class which would have deprived me of what is called a liberal education, it is not unlikely that, being strong in body, I should have taken to a way of life such as that in which my Pedlar passed the greater part of his days. At all events, I am here called upon freely to acknowledge that the character I have represented in his person is chiefly an idea of what I fancied my own character might have become in his circumstances.

[1] In *The Music of Humanity* (London, 1969), which appeared after this chapter was written, Jonathan Wordsworth argues for regarding *The Ruined Cottage* (the story of Margaret) and *The Pedlar* as separate poems from their inception at least through 1802, though Wordsworth throughout that time tried various ways of combining them. I have consistently regarded them as arrangements of a single poem, first called 'The Ruined Cottage', later (1801-2) 'The Pedlar'. Cf. *The Music of Humanity*, pp. 157 ff., 164-6, 245.

There is not a great deal of modesty in such an acknowledgement, for the Pedlar can be said to live in a world known only to himself and God, which is to live, without blasphemy, a God-like life.

Superficial resemblances between the situation in the early versions of 'The Ruined Cottage' and that in *The Rime of the Ancient Mariner*—the compulsive story-teller, the passive listener, a concluding passage (in one version) that brings absolution through the blessing of the creatures—only serve to bring out the deficiencies of 'The Ruined Cottage'.[1] Presumably because Wordsworth's interest in the poem was largely autobiographical, he was not fully able to decide upon the importance of the Pedlar's education, the centrality of the story of Margaret, or where the reader was to think of himself as having been when he came to the last line. Margaret, reduced by the burden of circumstance from a generous young wife blessed in comfort and peace to an apathetic widow, is made a perishable thing, less permanent than the ruined walls of her garden, as 'Her tattered clothes were ruffled by the wind / Even at the side of her own fire'. Margaret is, in what was at one time the last line of the poem, only the 'last human tenant of these ruined walls'.

But clearly, given Wordsworth's investment in the character of the Pedlar, the story could not be left there, and even in 1798 he tried several conclusions designed to place in some sort of harmony the story, its teller, and the poem's narrator. In one, resolution takes the form of a visual event, as the speaker looks again at the distressing scene and it resolves itself into 'Colours and forms of a strange discipline' that renders him a better and wiser man. In succeeding attempts at a conclusion the narrator ascribes his moral edification to the *words* the Pedlar has used for his story, or to his own act of looking *away* from the scene to consider the beautiful sunshine and the verdant green as an antidote and alternative. But the most ambitious conclusion was the last one Wordsworth tried in 1798, and it so altered the form of the poem that it perhaps accounts for his having then abandoned 'The Ruined Cottage' for several years. This ending, an argument later incorporated into book IV of *The Excursion*, takes the reader directly into the realm

---

[1] *Music of Humanity*, p. 98.

of reflective autobiography, as Pedlar and narrator and Margaret are all subsumed in the plural 'we' or the impersonal 'man' who has been taught to bear circumstance by loving 'such objects as excite no morbid passions'. For such a man, who then becomes 'we', an ideal education is outlined: our love for objects leads us by holy tenderness to seek the good and find the good we seek, our sense becomes subservient to moral purpose, and as a result 'no naked hearts, / No naked minds shall then be left to mourn / The burthen of existence'. Because our love relates all objects, even analytic science kindles our hearts, majestic imagery cannot dwindle to a barren picture, and the senses and intellect work in aid of one another.

Having set up this idealized psychology and ethic for man's relation to nature, to other men, and to knowledge, Wordsworth has the terms for describing what happens to story-teller and to listener: the Pedlar's words are not sound or letters, but a Meaning composed of the presence of his eye as well as his voice, and the narrator does not, listening, 'understand'—rather, his spirit obeys the Pedlar's meanings in a moment, or an hour, of timeless mysterious communion. At this point 'The Ruined Cottage' must of its own weight and multiplicity have sunk from sight, its growth since it was first begun in 1797 having made it an ungainly anthology of ideas rather than a poem. However well this ending may have helped Wordsworth to clarify his own relation to the concerns of the poem, it was, as he must have realized, dramatically disastrous. By April 1798 this long educational epilogue had been added, and he apparently did not return to the poem again until 1801. But even though he set it aside, he by no means forgot it.

In the late spring of 1798 Wordsworth composed several of the *Lyrical Ballads*, including 'The Idiot Boy', and wrote much of 'Peter Bell', just before he and Dorothy left Alfoxden on June 23rd, first for a week at Nether Stowey and then Shirehampton, near Bristol. In 'Tintern Abbey', written in the middle of July, Wordsworth again confronted exactly the questions that had made 'The Ruined Cottage' grow so unwieldy. Speaking in 'Tintern Abbey' by and for himself, he avoids the dramatic awkwardness of 'The Ruined Cottage', though he must of course speak with greater restraint about the virtues of the educated sensibility.

The poem opens modestly with the speaker insisting on no more than he can demonstrate: his presence, the scene, the time that has elapsed since his last visit. The immediacy of details is emphasized—these plots, these farms, these hedgerows—but in the first section the movement from visual apprehension to speculation is either unemphatic—'these steep and lofty cliffs, / That on a wild secluded scene impress / Thoughts of more deep seclusion'— or vaguely apologetic—wreathes of smoke 'from among the trees! / With some uncertain notice, as might seem / Of vagrant dwellers in the houseless woods.'

One of the interests in reading 'Tintern Abbey' is to watch the poet's gradual development toward a position from which more than this can be said, more emphatically. Experience clearly precedes theory as the narrator explains with deliberate care that the sensations recalled from his earlier visit (and they are explicitly sensations not visual memories), have earned their importance by having sustained him 'in lonely rooms, and 'mid the din / Of towns and cities'. Their utilitarian, therapeutic value is stated, their moral value only suggested—they 'may have had no trivial influence / On that best portion of a good man's life'. The additional benefit 'of aspect more sublime' that he owes to the forms of beauty is clearly an attribute of something other than the poet—the 'blessed mood, / In which the burthen of the mystery, / In which the heavy and the weary weight / Of all this unintelligible world, / Is lightened.' And here, as in the ending of 'The Ruined Cottage', the larger claims are made impersonally plural, for it is 'we', not he, who become a living soul, who 'see into the life of things'. Of course the shift of pronoun is partly responsible for shifting the tone from narrative to persuasive—the reader is less likely to question the nature of an experience he is told he shares—but in the doubting first person at the beginning of the third section the narrator seems to resume his pose of absolute honesty.

The situation at this point becomes more complex, for the 'I' who stands 'here' stands not in a place but in a moment of time, conditioned by his dim and faint recognitions of the past, soothed by his sense of present pleasure, filled with anticipations of this moment's usefulness in the future. And the *I* who stands here is not more constant than the place, for he was once the glad animal moving unthinking through coarse pleasures, then the young man who follows nature seeking with the urgency of fear to gratify the appetite, feeling, love, that was immediate and sensual. The goal he had then has no more precise name now because 'that time is past' with its aching joys or dizzy raptures, and a name can no longer signify because 'I cannot paint / What then I was.'

But the self now, here, is really no easier to paint. In fact, it offers a far greater challenge to the poet than the scene because his ear hears not the pure sound but blends reflection with apprehension and anticipation. The still sad music of humanity accompanies the vision. And to make this loss of singleness a gain, to explain belatedly the sense of alleviation, the meaning of which was assumed at the end of the second section, a new vocabulary must be found—the presence that disturbs with the joy of elevated thoughts (is the relationship causal or comparative?), the *sense* of something, a motion, a spirit (no name at all for this, and no location, or any name and all locations) 'whose dwelling is' (perhaps meaning, 'is like that produced by') the light of setting suns, round ocean, living air, blue sky, mind of man, and that acts by impelling and rolling. The 'therefore' that follows this confusing description obviously is not an introduction to a truth proven but a gesture of confidence in the face of the failure to have defined it satisfactorily. The mask of confidence leads to no better name for what he is now than it did for the causes of his being it: he is a well-pleased lover recognizing an anchor, a nurse, a guide, a guardian of the heart and the soul of his moral being. As Empson demonstrates in ways that are convincing in spite of the excessive number of his arguments, this is the weakest point in the poem.[1]

Perhaps just because he has failed to be clear the speaker turns, as does the speaker at the end of book II of *The Prelude*, to someone

[1] William Empson, *Seven Types of Ambiguity* (London, 1930), chapter IV.

else inside the poem to whom such things need not be explained,
as a dramatist might abruptly bring onto the stage a sympathetic
listener whose acceptance of the speaker precludes cynical and
awkward questions from the audience. In effect, Dorothy becomes
the anchor and nurse, a good shepherd indeed (for thou art with
me), and *deus ex machina*.

The double negatives and conditionals of the first three lines of
the last section seem almost deliberately confusing. Can they
mean, This teaching has encouraged me to allow the decay of my
genial spirits? No, but it is with some effort, and the rescuing of
the sentence's subject from the fourth line, that the lines are made
to read, Even if I had not been thus taught, your presence would
not have allowed my genial spirits to decay. The recovery from
confusion, in the syntax as well as the sense of the poem, depends
upon the poet's shifting attention to Dorothy's sensibility and on
the reader's willingness to forget a great deal of what he has been
told. Communication with Dorothy, like that with the Pedlar in
the last 1798 version of the ending of 'The Ruined Cottage', is not
a matter of words at all—her voice contains in fact the language of
his former heart, her eyes his former pleasures, and the person of
his sister replaces the confusion of the scene, as the Pedlar replaced the story of Margaret. The narrator's response to such
a moment of communion is not a statement but a prayer, addressed
to a Nature here even more powerful against the burthen of the
mystery than he had assumed before. The first part of that prayer
is one of the most moving moments in the poem:

> . . . let the moon
> Shine on thee in thy solitary walk;
> And let the misty mountain-winds be free
> To blow against thee . . .

But the tone of the prayer is always qualified by the speaker's
lack of confidence in its efficacy and in his role as supplicant.
Finally Dorothy is to remember, in addition to the forms, sounds
and harmonies of this scene, the brother who blesses and exhorts
her. Now it is not Nature or the educated heart but the poet
himself who is the source of healing thoughts, the nurse, anchor

and guide. The moment of their communication here, the impulse that brought him here, *his* warmer love, his 'far deeper zeal of holier love', are to be important finally because they are part of his service to her.

There are perhaps several ways to account for the dramatic shifting of subject in the last section of the poem. A lover's statement is not subject to any reader's demands for relational knowledge for it is by definition disarming; or, fear of loss and mortality is more easily consoled by human and domestic love than by devotion to a 'sense' or 'presence'; Dorothy is far more likely even than Nature not to betray the heart that loves her. Or perhaps it is enough to say that, like Coleridge, Wordsworth knew the strategy of introducing prayer when narrative becomes suspiciously unconvincing.[1]

Even if Wordsworth was convinced at the time that he had resolved the questions raised in 'Tintern Abbey' within the space of the poem, it is clear that he did not regard that poem as a very final statement about the nature of his own sensibility. He was never one to let a single example stand as a general demonstration. Nor was 'Tintern Abbey' a successful completion of all the interests he raised but could not settle in 'The Ruined Cottage'. The work begun at Goslar in the winter of 1798–9 was a return to the questions that perplexed him in both poems, now confronted in the context of a poem on his own life, a work of indefinite extent in which he would try to create and justify the voice that would, he assumed, eventually speak in *The Recluse*. By late 1799, when he temporarily suspended work on what would be called *The Prelude*, he had written a surprisingly self-contained poem of somewhat more than a thousand lines, some of them taken directly from 'The Ruined Cottage', all of them directed toward the unresolved questions of 'Tintern Abbey'.

The poem represented by MS. V, the revised fair copy of

[1] Geoffrey Hartman in *The Unmediated Vision* (New Haven, 1954) says that '*Wordsworth's understanding is characterized by the general absence of the will to attain relational knowledge*' (his italics), but here and in *Wordsworth's Poetry 1787–1814* he sees 'Tintern Abbey' as a more secure poem than I do. Thus the speaker's turn to Dorothy, which Hartman mentions in the second book, is seen as his attempt to overcome doubt about salvation rather than about poetic success.

books I and II probably written out in 1800 but representing the poem as it had been left in 1799, is a neat, economical, clear, chronological account of Wordsworth's education up to his eighteenth year. Most of the significant passages in this text appeared in the 1805 text as well, but several passages later distributed through books V and XI do, by their inclusion here, acquire surprisingly modified meanings.

For most of the thousand lines Wordsworth is concerned almost exclusively with the subject that permeated 'The Ruined Cottage' and 'Tintern Abbey'—the place of an attitude toward nature in the education of his own sensibility. The opening statement (in MS. V) declares the double purpose of self-definition and self-justification:

> Was it for this
> That one, the fairest of all Rivers lov'd
> To blend his murmurs with my Nurse's song
> And from his alder shades and rocky falls,
> And from his fords and shallows, sent a voice
> That flow'd along my dreams?

The preamble that provides an antecedent for the 'this' of the first line does not appear in any manuscript of the poem until 1804, so that *The Prelude* in all its early versions seems to take as its motive the providing of a referent for a pronoun without an antecedent, just as 'Tintern Abbey' can be said to question and redefine pronouns ('I') and adverbs ('here', 'now'). 'This', in the opening line, which can be a time, a man, a place, is a suitably ambiguous point from which to move backward through the history of a sensibility and the moments that have formed it. First appear in order the dramatic events of fair seed-time when the five year's child, the 'naked savage in a thunder-shower', is subjected to the vaguely sinister 'severer interventions' and palpable ministry of fearful natural retribution for childish thoughtless participation: the 'low breathings . . . and sounds of undistinguishable motion' that pursue the child who in plundering the woodcock's nest was 'in thought and wish . . . a fell destroyer'; the 'strange utterance' of the 'loud dry wind' that blew through the ears of the plunderer of the raven's nest; and of course the cliff that sent to the boy who had stolen the boat 'a dim and un-determined sense of unknown modes of being'. It is, says Words-worth, thanks to the wisdom and spirit of the universe that such forms and images, thus given breath and motion, build up the human soul, purify thought and feeling, '. . . sanctifying, by such discipline, / Both pain and fear, until we recognize / A grandeur in the beatings of the heart.' This mode of education, apparently because it comes as a shock demanding a response, Wordsworth finds superior to, or at least more effective than, that conducted through the medium of 'the vulgar words of man'. Hopefully, he assumes that having had the advantage of it he, or it (the distinction between himself and his talent is not vital) is not destined for trivial ends. When this reflection is followed by the account of the drowned man rising up from the water the incident is not, as it becomes when it is later placed in book V, an example of the power of literature to shield the sensitive mind against terror. Here instead terror is preserved unmodified and the incident is used partly to define more specifi-cally the use that can be made of nature's severer interventions, and leads directly to the explanation of spots of time (later relegated to book XI), those moments of sudden apprehension that have a 'fructifying Virtue whereby our minds (Especially the imaginative power) / Are nourished and invisibly repaired'. [MS. V]. The definition, with its two other examples—the visionary dreariness of the pool, beacon and woman; the sheep, blasted tree and stone well seen after his father's death—emphasize for the first time the active nature of the feeling man's response, and the uses he can make of the world without, in order to bring composition and consolation to the world within.

But lest nature's only service be seen as protection against those terrors she herself causes, Wordsworth hastens to explain that there are many occasions of unconscious intercourse leading to moments of simplicity, calm delight, the union of life and joy, in which the active mind of the perceiver lies open and fallow to the benignity of the universe. Severer interventions are carefully distinguished from events and moments that show 'How Nature by collateral interest, / And by extrinsic passion peopled first / My mind with forms or beautiful or grand.' Such moments are cherished precisely because they are isolated from the rest of life, and irrelevant to self. The boy watching the moon rise over the shepherds' huts '. . . stood, to images such as these, / A stranger, linking with the spectacle / No body of associated forms.' But the value of such events as cherished moments is finally vulgar compared to their effect on the heart, gained through constant repetition, which serves to 'impregnate and to elevate the mind'.

The distinctions among the various uses of nature are admittedly confusing, perhaps because they rely so heavily on the subjective degrees of the poet's consciousness at the moment of perception and during later reflection, and perhaps because the reader's most usual way of distinguishing among such moments on the page—the differences in their dramatic presentation—does not help him much in seeing Wordsworth's point. Indeed the poet himself is more than a little unsure about his clarity, for he suddenly addresses to Coleridge an apology for beginning so far back in his history with no excuse except self-indulgence—'the weakness of a human love, for days / Disown'd by memory'— and self-castigation—the hope 'that I might fetch / Reproaches from my former years whose power / May spur me on, in manhood now mature, / To honorable toil.' Obviously he was fascinated by the way his own mind worked, and its relevance to other minds is at best an afterthought.

Apparently having written and then for some reason torn out the flat opening of the second book, and having made several attempts to relate the excursions that will show dramatically the undramatic effect on him of the 'common range of visible things', Wordsworth gradually adopts an increasingly abstract vocabulary in accounting for the ecstasy of thoughtless moments when 'from excess / Of happiness, my blood appear'd to flow / With its own pleasure' and in accounting for the loss of ecstasy as the 'incidental charms' grew weaker and Nature became a goal rather than an 'intervenient' medium, when the sun ceased to be warmth and became a symbol, pledge and surety. But the adoption of an analytical vocabulary for autobiography is self-defeating, for the general habits, desires, thoughts of a particular place have no source available to science and reason, those analytical powers by which 'in weakness we create distinctions, then / Believe our puny boundaries are things / Which we perceive, and not which we have made.' Such distrust of reason, and of language, leads inevitably to a fundamental distrust of poetry and autobiography. Here indeed is restated the problem of the Pedlar knowing too much, of Wordsworth knowing too much about the Pedlar, of the poet's undeniable assurance of the significance of his own knowledge and his inability to convey it to a reader.

In the context of this poem, a way out seems to lie, for the moment, in a general discussion of apprehension in all children, not just himself. The infant babe, unlike the scientist (or the autobiographer), creates, unites, brings together his world, and 'all objects through all intercourse of sense'. As an inmate of an *active* (here and in 'The Ruined Cottage' Wordsworth italicizes the word) universe, the child acts as agent for the great creator, his mind works 'but in alliance with the works / Which it beholds.' But having given unconscious or pre-conscious apprehension so large a role and so exalted a position among human activities in general, he must consequently show how in his own particular case certain aspects of this sensibility have been sustained and augmented in spite of the fact that 'a trouble came into my mind / From unknown causes' so that 'I was left alone, / Seeking the visible world, nor knowing why.' The tone of authoritative certainty that was possible, if not totally persuasive, in the limited instance of 'Tintern Abbey' has here almost given way to the lyric doubt of 'The Rainbow'.

At first the lapsed state seems somehow a compensation. Now his mind lies open 'to Nature's finer influxes' and habit makes possible 'that more exact / And intimate communion which our hearts / Maintain with the minuter properties / Of objects which already are belov'd, / And of those only.' And so,

> The seasons came
> And every season brought a countless store
> Of modes and temporary qualities
> Which, but for this most watchful power of love

> Had been neglected, left a register
> Of permanent relations, else unknown,
> Hence life, and change, and beauty, solitude
> More active, even, than 'best society',
> Society made sweet as solitude
> By silent inobtrusive sympathies,
> And gentle agitations of the mind
> From manifold distinctions, difference
> Perceived in things, where to the common eye,
> No difference is; and hence, from the same source
> Sublimer joy . . .

The repeated 'hence' is an evasion of course, like the 'therefore' in the third section of 'Tintern Abbey', for such an argument can hardly lead to such a conclusion. And Wordsworth not surprisingly again shifts his terms, insisting that these moments have nothing to do with 'our purer mind / And intellectual life' but are the soul's memories of times when 'Remembering how she felt, but what she felt / Remembering not' the soul 'retains an obscure sense / Of possible sublimity.' Then the explanation becomes increasingly mechanical, and less believable. The creative sensibility sustained, immune to the regular attrition of the world, works in conjunction with the 'auxiliar light' from the mind to bestow splendour on the setting sun, birds, breezes, fountains, midnight storms. And again a repeated 'hence' is the sign that no explanation has been offered: 'Hence my obeisance, my devotion hence, / And hence my transport.'

Why should he insist so on the existence of a world in which the 'sentiment of Being' permeates everything? Why should the poet of *The Prelude* and the Pedlar of 'The Ruined Cottage' spend so much time evoking it? Presumably because this world is what was *not* seen, or seen only during moments that were in effect out of time, or at least seen only by a person who no longer sees them. It is the gift of cataracts, mountains, lakes to sustain and preserve his own sensibility in a world drastically different and palpably present, during a time of disillusionment, selfishness, fear, melancholy, waste of hopes o'erthrown, indifference, apathy, wicked exultation, sneers on visionary minds, dereliction, dismay. Like the dissolution of Margaret and her cottage, the fallen world here inevitably leads the poet once again to change his subject. The complimentary farewell to Coleridge as a man among few who will understand all this, is an appeal and a gesture of frustration. However articulately he can express in the dramatic juxtaposition of moments and images the relationship between unbearable knowledge, fear or guilt, and the saving restorative power of his own poetic sensibility apprehending in a richer way the world in which such knowledge has sway, it is an impossible task to elevate such apprehensions into an abstract definition of himself and a justification of his vocation as a poet.

It is easy to see why Wordsworth might have abandoned this poem, and 'The Ruined Cottage', at this point in their composition. But it is also easy to see why he must inevitably have felt the necessity of reassuming their burden, and why later, in 1802, he may have attempted to go on by turning from the impossibly solemn passages to the mock heroic wit of book III, and finally why he again laid aside *The Prelude* and went back to 'The Ruined Cottage' as a less personal confrontation of the questions on which both poems had foundered. The questions were ones that had to be solved if he was to go on as a poet, but the idiom in which the questions had so far been stated apparently made their resolution impossible. The burden of decision, the necessity of moving in some direction and the impossibility of finding any in which to move, faced Wordsworth in every important aspect of his life as a man and a poet during this new year of 1802.

Most simply, it seemed to be a question of whether or not he could tell himself the truth. Notions of beneficial nature seemed to be as illusory as his hopes for becoming a great public poet. In spite of being unable quite to say what it was that kept him going, in spite of the fact that everything that could be *said* seemed to deny any optimism, and all his rhetoric finally amounted to little that could stand the test of analytical reason, Wordsworth obviously felt that somehow his existence and vocation should be justifiable, and that the present all this past had gone to create had an expressible virtue. And if he could find little to justify faith in himself, there was at least an obligation to the loyalty of

Coleridge and Dorothy. The question was one of form as much as content: to know was to write, to find successful poetic statement was to justify his own being. The truth, if it could be found, would be the truth of art as well as self. Even when the form set the question outside himself, as in 'Peter Bell', Wordsworth seems to have been dissatisfied with the resolution, perhaps because Peter seemed too easy a way of dodging William.

(v)

So at the close of 1801, when winter brought an end to the constant visitors to Town End and even Coleridge was in London, Wordsworth went to work again on the poems that had been perplexing him for several years. The ways, if not the order, in which Wordsworth resumed work on 'The Ruined Cottage' in the winter of 1801–2 are fairly easily determined from the manuscripts surviving. The obvious change, of course, is the specific identity given to the narrator of Margaret's story. Apparently relying on the description of James Patrick that Sara Hutchinson sent him at the end of January and on her descriptions of him in conversations, Wordsworth changed 'Armytage' to make the story-teller conform to her memories of the 'intellectual Pedlar' of Kendal, who had married Sara's cousin and had given Sara a home for several years of her childhood. The new pedlar, Wordsworth told Isabella Fenwick many years later, was a happy discovery:

My own imaginations I was happy to find clothed in reality, and fresh ones suggested, by what [Sara] reported of this man's tenderness of heart, his strong and pure imagination, and his solid attainments in literature, chiefly religious whether in prose or verse.

Since there is no way of knowing what was contained either in Sara's 'very interesting account' or in her conversations, it is impossible to know how many of Wordsworth's changes were dictated by new information and how many were the product of his dissatisfaction with the poem as he had left it in 1798. Whatever his motive, it was obviously the work done early in 1802

that enabled Wordsworth to free the poem's narrator from himself, and to move decisively toward the kind of objective figure
who, after more transformations and another poem, appeared in
May as the Leechgatherer. And just as obviously, facts helped him
in achieving that independence. Names—'Patrick' and 'Drum-
mond'—and places—Perthshire, later Athol—and details—the
tiny, fair-faced girl, the older brother—appear frequently and
irrelevantly in the 1802 addenda to MS. B (of 1798), but are
eliminated in the draft of 1802 (MS. E) and subsequently. Whereas
in the 1798 version Wordsworth repeatedly used statements
about the Pedlar that he was later to apply to himself in *The
Prelude*, now Patrick's background is made distinctively Scottish,
as Wordsworth emphasizes the austerity of life and religion in
Scotland, and carefully distinguishes it from that of English life
(and his own). And such facts lead to new kinds of statements.
Although the word 'fear' first appears in this context in the later
MS. M as the antagonist of love, the appearance of love in MS. E
is not spontaneous (as in MS. B), not merely Nature's way of
counteracting 'gloomy notions' (as in the first 1802 addendum),
but comes about to modify the educational effect of tales of

> The life and death of martyrs, who sustained,
> Intolerable pangs, the cruel time
> Of superstition and the Covenant
> That like an echo rings through Scotland still.   (MS. E$_2$)

Perhaps Wordsworth gave the clearest indication of his freedom
from the Pedlar by making him for the first time in the latest of the
1802 revisions (MS. E$_2$) a poet-manqué:

> Oh! many are the Poets that are sown
> By Nature; men endowed with highest gifts,
> The vision and the faculty divine;
> Yet wanting the accomplishment of verse,
> And never being led by accident
> Or circumstance to take unto the height
> (By estimate comparative at least)
> The measure of themselves, live out their time,
> Husbanding that which they possess within,
> And go to the grave unthought of.

Though few claims can be made for the excellence of the verse or
the originality of its sentiment, such a statement requires (as it did
in Gray's *Elegy*) a poet's clear sense of his own calling and the
acceptance of his distance from and superiority to the Natural man
of sensitivity. As he revised 'The Ruined Cottage', this way of
defining the poem's other narrator must have given Wordsworth
his justification for being present as an additional voice. He is now
a spokesman, because of his office as poet, for the articulate but
unliterary poet-manqué:

> And some small portion of his eloquent speech,
> And something that may serve to set in view
> The feeling pleasures of his loneliness . . .
>   . . . I will here record in verse.

By severing the poet from the man of intense feeling, himself
from the Pedlar, Wordsworth indirectly defines a role for the poet
that includes more than coming to terms with his own heritage.
The poet is not only the explorer of the origins and obligations of
his own genius, but a craftsman who supplies written words for
the insights of extraordinary men who would otherwise pass
silently from the world. Such men are their own justification, and
the poet achieves his by recognizing and re-creating them. By
being a translator, the poet sets his own house in order in a
manner he does not have to understand fully, or explain. For the
time being, such dependence on the perceptions and virtues of
others did not bother him.

The relation of poet to Pedlar was obviously the largest and
most difficult legacy left to Wordsworth by his work on the
poem three and a half years earlier. This question, which is also the
question of how the poem is to be ended, and how Margaret's
history is to be seen and borne, preoccupied Wordsworth throughout the winter of 1801–2. The surviving manuscripts show no
other changes that in extent or intensity could account for the
pain that, Dorothy tells us, these revisions cost her brother. In
order finally to conclude the poem, Wordsworth returned to the
first few lines of his first alternate 1798 ending:

> The old man ceased: he saw that I was moved.
> From that low bench rising instinctively
> I turned away in weakness . . .

This time, because of the greater importance that has been given to the Pedlar throughout the poem, the poet has other resources to turn to, and need not simply conclude that he has been subjected to 'a strange discipline' which has rendered him a better and a wiser man. The difficulty of feeling and saying this time is directly faced: Margaret's history

> . . . seemed
> To comfort me while with a brother's love
> I blessed her in the impotence of grief.

The necessity of eventually confronting a moment such as this has been anticipated throughout the revised poem. Patrick's greatest virtue, for instance, is not his susceptibility to natural impressions (though he has that) but his fortitude. As he began to tell the story of Margaret, he told his listener (in language that anticipates the 'Essay on Epitaphs') that an elegaic poet asking the stones to mourn is not being fanciful but speaks 'in a voice / Obedient to the strong creative power / Of human passion'. And Patrick, Wordsworth reminds his reader,

> . . . was alive
> To all that was enjoyed where'er he went,
> And all that was endured; for, in himself
> Happy, and quiet in his cheerfulness,
> He had no painful pressure from without
> That made him turn aside from wretchedness
> With coward fears. He could *afford* to suffer
> With those whom he saw suffer.

Simultaneously to bless and to be comforted, to act and be acted upon—these are the achievements of the Pedlar and, if a conclusion can be found, the burden of the Pedlar's story and the mode by which human passion can be made strongly creative and attain a voice. But this, perhaps, is too much to expect. Having blessed Margaret impotently, the speaker returns to trace 'fondly'

That secret spirit of humanity
Which, 'mid the calm oblivious tendencies
Of nature, 'mid her plants, and weeds, and flowers,
And silent overgrowings, still survived.

Finally, there is no more for the Pedlar to say, or the speaker to learn, than in the third alternate ending of three years before:

... that heavenly consolation springs,
From sources deeper far than deepest pain,
For the meek suffer.

Grief cannot live where 'meditation' is. The centre on which the poem turns is, still, finally, empty, and destined to remain that way forever, although in 1845 Faith and the Cross were rather crudely inserted to disguise the gap. The otherness of the Pedlar has been established, but the poem still was not finished. Although Dorothy's last reference to William's work on the poem refers also to his plan for publishing it along with 'Peter Bell', it was nevertheless set aside, probably until 1804, when Wordsworth, now seeing it as the first stage of a longer excursion, need no longer worry about his temptations to expand it beyond narrative.

(vi)

Perhaps with a sense of satisfaction with his revisions of 'The Ruined Cottage' (now 'The Pedlar'), perhaps out of frustration, perhaps even as a preparation for Coleridge's imminent return north, Wordsworth began early in March to turn his attention to kinds of composition ostensibly very different from those with which he had been occupied. On March 7th he returned to Grasmere after a four-day trip, the destination and purpose of which is not clear from Dorothy's *Journal* except that his itinerary included Keswick and he returned 'a little fatigued with reading his poems'. With him he brought two new stanzas of 'Ruth', which Dorothy had been copying out that morning (along with stitching up 'The Pedlar', completed just before William left). As he added to 'Ruth', Wordsworth apparently turned his attention to the composition of further, similar ballads of poverty, desertion and loss. On March 11th and 12th he worked at 'The Singing Bird' (later 'The Sailor's Mother'), the story of a majestic woman carrying, with strength and dignity, the caged bird which is her only legacy from her lost sailor son. On March 13th, Dorothy relates, 'William finished "Alice Fell", and then he wrote the poem of "The Beggar Woman" '. The second of these, like 'The Singing Bird' (which shares its stanza and meter), is again the story of a woman's majesty preserved in adversity and poverty (modified to be sure by the wild free exuberance of her children's lies); and, like 'Alice Fell', it is the retelling of a story recorded in Dorothy's *Journal* ('The Beggar Woman': 27 May 1800; 'Alice Fell': 16 February 1802). Finally on March 16th and 17th Wordsworth wrote out the story of the emigrant mother who attaches herself to an English child to replace the one she has left behind in France, and sings a lullaby to him which Wordsworth pretends to transcribe in English. The fact that Wordsworth later remembered this poem as having been written in 1802 during a visit to Mary and her brother at Sockburn (which they had left in 1800) implies at least that he associated the poem's composition with Mary's company, and may suggest that Wordsworth visited Mary, perhaps at Penrith or even Gallow Hill, during his trip the fortnight before.

The group of ballads, in their shared concern with the distress of forsaken women and children, and their majesty or despair in the face of adversity, of course echo in form and substance the sort of thing Wordsworth had included in the first volume of *Lyrical Ballads* four years before, and they share a preoccupation, if not a form, with the extensive work he had been doing on 'The Pedlar'. But more suggestive, and less clear, is the connection between these poems and his own new emerging relation to Annette and Mary. He can hardly have been unconscious of his own partial resemblance to the sprightly feckless young man in 'Ruth', of Annette's resemblance to the distressed emigrant mother, the resemblance even of Caroline's state to that of Alice Fell (who must have been about the same age). None of the three poems, of course, relates any part of Wordsworth's own story, and all have sources outside his relation with Annette. But all

three can be seen as alternative ways of viewing his own experience, or attempts to understand other consequences his action
could have had. Mary Moorman has pointed out the resemblance
between the language of 'The Mad Mother' (1798) and one of
Annette's undelivered letters, and suggests that other similar
letters from Annette, along with William's own sense of responsibility, must have given to the 1798 ballads of deserted
women 'a sharpness of realism that they would not otherwise
have possessed' (Moorman, I., 385). So it is entirely understandable that the resumed correspondence with Annette,
especially now that William has determined to marry, should
coincide with a renewed interest in such ballads. But 'interest',
rather than expiation or apology, may be the limit of Wordsworth's personal involvement.

In any case, during the same week in March Wordsworth
embarked on a new and very different form of poetry. On March
14th he began 'The Butterfly', and worked on it and 'The Cuckoo'
during the following week—a week that began with Coleridge's
first visit to Grasmere in four months and ended with the composition of the first four stanzas of the 'Immortality' Ode. The
personal perplexities of that week must have been enormous.
Between the Sunday Coleridge left them and the following
Sunday when William and Dorothy rejoined him at Keswick,
they 'talked a good deal about C. and other interesting things'
with some conclusive results: on Monday 'We' (Dorothy's use of
this pronoun for a decision properly William's is characteristic)
'resolved to see Annette, and that Wm. should go to Mary'.
Dorothy's frequent allusions to her poor health, in the entries for
Wednesday, Thursday, Friday, Sunday and most of the following
week, indicate the distress to which she was prone when her
brother was faced with decisive actions. And other indices to the
inner activity of the household abound: during the week Dorothy
wrote at least two letters to Sara and Mary Hutchinson, one to
her brother Richard; William wrote once to Coleridge and once
to Annette; and the Wordsworths received two letters from Mary,
two from Sara, and of course the one from 'poor Annette' on
Monday that seems to have prompted 'their' resolution.

What is most surprising about the poems William worked on
during that week in March is the immediacy of the object or
situation with which they begin, and the absence of any narrative
at all. 'The Cuckoo', 'The Butterfly' and 'The Silver How poem'
(presumably VI in the 'Poems on the Naming of Places') assume
an intimate audience that does not need to be given a personal or
narrative context. In all three, for instance, the initial contemplation of an object, place or sound provides an occasion to be
retrospective ('in my school-boy days', 'Oh! pleasant, pleasant
were the days', 'When once again we met in Grasmere Vale').
The poet seeks, at times desperately, to rediscover in the present
object and its continuity with the past a parallel continuity in his
own response to mystery. The forest grove in which John walked
offers little help toward such discoveries:

> Alone I tread this path;—for aught I know,
> Timing my steps to thine; and, with a store
> Of undistinguishable sympathies,
> Mingling most earnest wishes for the day
> When we, and others whom we love, shall meet
> A second time, in Grasmere's happy Vale.

And although the conclusion is clearly enough Wordsworth's,
the earlier descriptive language is another of those baffling in-
stances of a poem echoing Dorothy's *Journal* (for February 23rd),
or Dorothy perhaps echoing the initial perceptions of her brother.
The cuckoo in the vale of visionary hours offers little more
opportunity for distinguishing the sympathies that gather round
'an invisible thing, a voice, a mystery'. 'Thou wert still a hope, a
love; / Still longed for, never seen!'

The closest antecedents for poems such as these are the short
untitled poem beginning 'A whirl-blast from behind the hill',
written in March 1798 but not published until the second edition
of *Lyrical Ballads*, in a form that was later altered, and 'The
Sparrow's Nest', composed sometime in 1801. The scene in the
earlier poem is an 'undergrove' of holly trees which forms a
protective bower within an oak grove during a hailstorm. In the
stillness after a blast of wind the hailstones cause the fallen but

green holly leaves to 'jump up and spring / As if each were a living thing' (MS.). The appearance of life in a dead object (Robin Goodfellow is a later addition) is, in the versions of the poem published from 1800 to 1805, the occasion of a final four line appeal:

> Oh! grant me Heaven a heart at ease,
> That I may never cease to find,
> Even in appearances like these,
> Enough to nourish and to stir my mind.

The anticipation of 'Daffodils', 'The Rainbow', even the 'Immortality' Ode, is obvious when the conclusion is added to the original apprehension, and the quest behind the observation is made explicit. As Bateson says, the new tone of the poems of 1802 is in part due to Wordsworth having adopted his sister's interest in the apprehension of small particularity, and the objects observed in these poems of 1802 do indeed become noticeably smaller (cf. Bateson, pp. 159–60). The eggs in the sparrow's nest are not in themselves remarkable, but they recall a sparrow's nest near his father's house that he and Dorothy visited as children, which in turn is a reminder that he still has the blessing of Dorothy's company:

> She gave me eyes, she gave me ears;
> And humble cares, and delicate fears;
> A heart, the fountain of sweet tears;
> And love, and thought, and joy.

In April 1802 Dorothy, writing to Mary Hutchinson, urged upon her the counsel she had with apparent success given her brother: 'Study the flowers, the birds and all the common things that are about you . . . and do not make loving us your business, but let your love of us make up the spirit of all the business you have.'

It is clear that Dorothy's role in influencing the directions that her brother's sensibility took had been constant and unequivocal, and that they both understood its significance in similar terms. But the rather sudden and exclusive attention he gave to this mode of perception and composition in 1802 was obviously his own choice, his own determination now to use this means of seeking nourishment and enlightenment. In 'The Pedlar' he had depended on his creation of a perceiver outside himself, distanced by narrative, but even there abstract rhetoric seemed to be the only way to move from story to meaning. Looking closely at an object, something smaller and more self-evidently symbolic than a ruined cottage, was an alternative. If the justification for a whole sensibility required an autobiography or narrative that he could not finish, an isolated moment of time in which attention is ostensibly directed toward one of the 'common things' might be self-explanatory.

Whatever Wordsworth had to say, now, in March of 1802, he had known for several years. In fact, if his 'subject' were not virtually common knowledge, no reader would be able to make much sense of these poems. What distinguishes them and their successors is not what they have to say, but the pressure behind them, the communicated sense of the poet's overriding need to find a way to speak so that the mode of composition itself will alleviate that pressure.

In part because it seems to have given Wordsworth a great deal of trouble, 'To a Butterfly' is one of the most interesting of the poems composed during this week in March; and at some stage in their composition the two poems finally given this title may well have been a single poem. Although in publishing them Wordsworth was always careful to separate them ('Stay near me' and 'I've watched you now' appearing at opposite ends of the collection called 'Moods of my own Mind'), and sent them as separate poems to the Hutchinsons in May, Dorothy's *Journal* is ambiguous about their separation. On March 14th she notes that 'while we were at breakfast ... he wrote the poem "To a Butterfly!" ' but apparently was unsatisfied for at bedtime 'he began to try to alter "The Butterfly" '. Ten days later, on March 24th, Dorothy records that 'Wm. altered "The Butterfly" as we came from Rydale'. A butterfly poem is not mentioned again until April 20th when 'William wrote a conclusion to the poem of the Butterfly—"I've watched you now a full half hour." ' Although Helen Darbishire assumes that Dorothy quotes the opening line in order to distinguish between the two poems, she may just as reasonably be assumed to be indicating how the conclusion began —particularly since she refers to *the*, not *another*, poem about a butterfly. Other evidence as well suggests that the four stanzas, though printed as two poems, have rather close ties. In the Meyerstein (Longman) manuscript of the poems submitted to the publishers for the 1807 volume, the first poem is clearly written, in Dorothy's hand, on a single sheet of paper, with some alterations in the text, thus:

> Stay near me—do not take thy flight!
> A little longer stay in sight!
> -Pleased am I to converse with thee [cancelled]
> Much converse do I find in thee
> Historian of my infancy.
> Float near me; do not yet depart
> Dead times revive in thee:
> Thou bright, gay creature as thou art!
> A solemn image to my heart,
> My father's family!
>
> Oh pleasant, pleasant were the days
> The time, when in our childish plays
> My sister Dorothy [cancelled] Emma [?cancelled?]
>   [Emmeline and I]
> Together chaced the Butterfly!
> A very hunter did I rush
> Upon the prey:—with leaps and springs
> I followed on from brake to bush;
> But She, God love her! feared to brush
> The dust from off its wings.

The changes in these two stanzas are substantive enough to suggest that the lines were written out fairly early. A version that Coleridge sent to Poole on May 7th reads much as this manuscript: 'historian' is still the word in line 4, and 'Emmeline' has replaced 'Dorothy' and 'Emma'. However, another manuscript version of the poem sent to the Hutchinsons in late May is confusingly different. Its second line reads 'a little moment stay in sight' (clearly earlier than the Meyerstein MS.); its third line is 'Much *reading* do I find in thee', where the idea of conversation has apparently not yet suggested itself but where, paradoxically, the form 'Much . . . do I find' seems a good deal *later* than the cancelled line 'Pleased am I . . .' in the Meyerstein MS.; yet, again, 'Bible' in the fourth line of the Hutchinson MS. rather obviously antedates 'Historian'. It is of course probable that the version sent to the Hutchinsons is earlier than the Meyerstein MS., may indeed be the words written out on March 14th. But it is almost as clear that the text sent to Longman in 1807 is, before the revisions were made for publication, almost contemporary with it—recording as it does the discovery of the word 'converse', its use first as a verb and then, reverting to the original syntax, as a noun.

The second Butterfly poem has an even odder appearance in the manuscript sent to Longman. In Dorothy's hand again, though in letters somewhat larger than usual, appears the stanza:

> I've watched you now a full half hour,
> Self-poised upon that yellow flower;
> And, little Butterfly! indeed
> I know not if you sleep or feed.
> How motionless! not frozen seas
> More motionless! and then
> What joy awaits you, when the breeze
> Shall find you out among the trees,
> And call you forth again.

Then, stitched loosely with thread to the half-sheet on which these words appear, is another half-sheet, again in Dorothy's hand but with writing of a size and placement on the page far more like that of the earlier two stanzas:

> This plot of Orchard ground is ours;
> My trees they are, my Sister's flowers;
> Stop here whenever you are weary,
> And feed as in a sanctuary!
> Come often to us, fear no wrong;
> Sit near us on the bough!
> We'll talk of sunshine and of song;

And childish Summer days, that were as long
As twenty days are now.

Any reconstruction of the movements of a poet's mind in the
act of composition must be wildly speculative, especially when it
is based on manuscript evidence as slight or as confusing as this,
but there does seem internal and external evidence to suggest that at
some time early in the composition there may have been a single
Butterfly poem, including at least some version of the first two
stanzas (i.e. the first poem) and probably the last stanza of the
second. This assumed poem would have been remarkably consistent in tone and attitude. When the insect appears, it is greeted
with a whimsical invitation. But the social tone, and the insect,
disappear when the butterfly becomes a solemn image of the past.
And accompanying the nostalgia, as so often in *The Prelude*, is
remorse for guilty violence committed against nature, with
Dorothy's presence as an admonishment: The very hunter rushing
upon the prey is set against the gentle child who feared to brush its
wings. In the 'God love her!' indeed there is as much apology to
Dorothy as to the butterfly.

If the movement set up by these two stanzas were followed by
the nine lines comprising the second stanza of the second poem, a
small drama would be created. Recompense for past injustice
would be made by generous hospitality. To be sure, the social
gestures through which a return to the present is achieved would
be playful and quietly mocking, as the condescending host
offers, with some wit, to provide refuge, sanctuary, and friendly
companionship. The repentant boy, now become a man, and
head of a household, together with his still gentle sister, create in
the present an apology for past thoughtlessness. The solemnity
of the first image (the first name for the butterfly was Bible) is
alleviated by gentle humour.

The appearance of an object in nature, its transformation into
an admonishing reminder of a guilty past, and the attempt by the
poet, as he steps forward into the present, to offer contrition and
explanation is a pattern so familiar to the reader of Wordsworth
that once it is seen here it is difficult to imagine the sense of those
first two stanzas without this conclusion and resolution. And it is

equally difficult, looking just at the two stanzas making up the
second poem, to imagine how the poet moved from the first one
of them to the second, if they stand alone.

But if 'To a Butterfly' did begin as a three stanza poem similar
to the one imagined together above, something presumably was
missing—and the existence now of a stanza beginning 'I've
watched you' makes it fairly easy to see what that something may
have been. In the three stanza poem, of course, there is no butterfly,
no object, insect, thing—there is only a solemn image, Bible,
historian, or wronged guest. But the whole stanza beginning
'I've watched you now' insists on the remoteness, otherness,
mysteriousness of the butterfly as a butterfly, an aspect of nature
as alien as frozen seas. In this stanza there is no image-making,
no condescension, no whimsy, little except a bewilderment
reflected in language and tone far different from that of the other
stanzas. If Dorothy means that this stanza alone was indeed a
conclusion to a single poem about a butterfly, and if it once stood
after the stanza it now precedes (or some version of that stanza),
one can see why Wordsworth might once have put it there, and
why its difference in tone made it impossible to keep it there.
Then perhaps it was made the second last stanza in a four stanza
poem—the breeze which called it forth being the occasion for a
second invitation called after it, as it were. And finally, the tone
still jarring, the stanza dedicated to the alien nature of the butterfly still interrupting the drama neatly represented by stanzas 1, 2
and 4, perhaps Wordsworth simply abandoned the idea of a
dramatic poem entirely and, making the best of his failure to fit it
all together, separated the stanzas into two different if inconclusive
poems and, in all printed versions, placed them as far apart as he
could.

Whatever its original text, the Butterfly poem—or poems—
shares with 'The Cuckoo' a nostalgia for a lost golden time that
'The Sparrow's Nest', written a year before, does not suggest, but
in its whimsical repentance, 'To a Butterfly' is unique. The manuscript revisions and Dorothy's comments show that attempts were
made on a number of occasions to get 'The Butterfly' right,
whether or not the revisions followed the elaborate order I have

imagined. Such a concern with what must at first seem a rather innocuous poem certainly implies that more was involved here than finally reached the words of any of its versions. The four stanzas put side by side comprise what in retrospect can be seen as a pattern: a whimsical greeting is extended, as the object becomes an image it is an occasion for indulging nostalgic recollections. Then when the image reasserts its mysterious but undeniable present reality, the speaker asserts his ability to master this otherness by a partly witty gesture of condescension. The pattern is rather overbearing for this poem, but within a few weeks it will reappear in a far finer and more self-conscious tone in 'Resolution and Independence', where there is no hedging about guilt and misery, and the drama is fully expressed and finally resolved.

The poems about John's Grove, the Cuckoo, and the first two Butterfly stanzas do set past against present in a manner that leads almost inevitably to the wish for natural piety as a binding continuity, expressed a few days later at the end of 'The Rainbow', and to the opening stanzas of the 'Immortality' Ode that followed 'The Rainbow' within a few hours. All these poems begin to imply the necessity for shoring fragments against an uncertain future, when attempts at self-justification have failed; as yet, 'The Ruined Cottage' ('The Pedlar') and 'Peter Bell' were not finished, 'Home at Grasmere' and the early passages for *The Prelude* were a long way from being fulfilled as *The Recluse*, and Wordsworth seems to have been far less certain than he was at the end of 1800 about what course his literary career should take, what sort of poetry he should write.

When Coleridge reprinted 'The Rainbow' in Essay V of the General Introduction to *The Friend*, the terms he used to introduce it were psychological and startlingly modern. Deriding men who cannot, by contemplating their past in the present, 'produce . . . continuity in their self-consciousness', he finds that they 'exist in fragments'. 'Annihilated as to the past, they are dead to the future, or seek for the proofs of it everywhere, only not (where they alone can be found) in themselves.' Yet the tone of Wordsworth's conclusion to 'The Rainbow' implies that at the time he feared he was one of those whom Coleridge now scorned. The last lines are self-protecting and reassuring, but certainly not triumphant. It was on Friday night, March 26th, Dorothy notes, 'while I was getting into bed', that William wrote 'The Rainbow'. And in view of his other poetic activities during the week it is perhaps less astonishing that the poem should have seemed to Dorothy to burst forth in a few moments, complete even to title, for it is a summary, this time in general terms, of the questions and perplexities underlying his dogged efforts at other compositions of that week. That it was not in any sense a solution is best indicated by the fact that two months later, on May 14th, Wordsworth was still 'haunted with altering' it. Since no manuscript version exists of any of that week's poems earlier than the collection sent to the Hutchinsons late in May, it must be assumed that, except for its last line, 'The Rainbow' stood as it does now on the 'divine morning' of Saturday, March 27th. And the fact that William at breakfast that morning wrote 'part of an ode' certainly implies that something very similar to the present version of 'The Rainbow' had been completed.

If the 'part of an ode' did comprise some version of the first four stanzas of the 'Immortality' Ode, like 'The Rainbow', it set a question rather than achieved a resolution. The source of the lines—their possible echoes of Burnet, 'The Mad Monk', Fénelon or Coleridge—is not as immediately important as their precision, their confidence, their honesty and courage and forthrightness about the limits of certainty. The loss, alienation or fear at which Wordsworth had only hinted delicately in the poems he worked on earlier in the week are here exposed defiantly: 'There was a time', but 'The Things which I have seen I now can see no more'. Fear is faced resolutely, and the abrupt turn to the present is dramatic because it is deliberate, because prosaic verse is suddenly obliterated by song that is the more real and the more moving for the flatness of what has preceded it:

> The Rainbow comes and goes,
> And lovely is the rose.

This sudden lyric cry, an interposition of the imagination indeed though hardly a shadowy one, permits some equanimity in the speaker's confrontation of past and present. Loss is openly acknowledged. Whatever the 'timely utterance' may have been that gave relief to 'that thought of grief' that 'came to me alone'—it may as likely have been the turn in the first stanza of this poem as 'The Rainbow'—its consequence is strength rather than consolation. The imperative address to the shepherd boy ('Shout round me'), the blessing of the creatures, the poet's insistence on his own participation in all that lies about him—I have heard, I see, I feel—I feel it all, I hear, I hear, with joy I hear—appear as resolute willed acts inspired by the militant trumpets of the cataract. A cancelled earlier reading of the sixth line of the fourth stanza, preserved in MS. M and still legible in the Meyerstein manuscript, brings this stridency to the verge of incontinence: 'Even yet more gladness—I can hold it all.' In all versions of the poem, of course, the enthusiasm is too violent and insistent, for imagination has allowed reason to speak her own language far too soon and too easily, as the apparition of the single tree makes clear. The stanzas end, as far as argument is concerned, where they began. But they end here with a difference that Coleridge must have perceived painfully when he heard the verse the following week, most probably on Sunday, April 4th, during William and Dorothy's week at Keswick. In these four stanzas the nervous self-protection of the poems Wordsworth composed earlier in that March week has yielded to a freedom and strength that allows particular moments to be fully realized, that allows, in other words, drama to replace easy wit or easier generalization. Because the poet has dramatized moments of strength, the reader can see the moments of weakness as something more than self-pity. 'Dramatic' to be sure is an awkward word to use to describe lines replete with generalization, description, pathetic fallacy, and most of the rhetorical conventions of the eighteenth-century nature poem. But the reader is certainly asked to respond to shifts of tone, intensity and volume in the speaker's voice as he moves from one mode and mood to another, from prosaic complaint to lyrical song to insistent joyous enthusiasm, from distance to participation to terrified singular alienation. If the mood rather than its cause is taken to be the concern of the poem, the vagueness of objects, scenes and sounds is irrelevant. In

'The Rainbow' time, doctrine and mood are so oddly combined that the poem does seem to express the poet's unrealized self-deception, but in the opening of the Ode the poet is far more clearly assured of his direction and his response to it. The shadowy interposition of the imagination guides as effectively as it binds the speaker. Composition, the setting in comprehensible order and harmony of the poet's response, makes less relevant the fact that nothing is communicated 'about' the world in which the response takes place or the life of the respondent.

No solution is found in the opening of the 'Immortality' Ode, no argument resolves the paradox that sensation has created, but a new mode of stating an essential question has been discovered. And presumably it was the mode of this poem, its ability, through its form, to communicate the sense of pressure, that so affected Coleridge that he replied with the first version of 'Dejection'. He too takes up the common pre-occupation with the loss of feeling response, poetic anaesthesia as it were, and responding to the sense of urgency Wordsworth has communicated so well, characteristically applies it to his own private perplexities. The relationship between Wordsworth's art and his life in the spring of 1802 is inescapable but finally mystifying—the shadowy interposition of the imagination so transforms the language of personal perplexity into poetic uncertainty that the biographer can only say that here art and life share an urgency rather than a subject.

In a way, Wordsworth is about to abandon the indulgence in visionary hours that the call of the cuckoo has invited or the sight of the butterfly provoked. The expression and control of immediate anxiety is a far more compelling motive, and one that can best be carried out in the present rather than in the narrative past. The opening of the 'Immortality' Ode represents the laying aside of defences—narrative, whimsy, abstract rhetoric, a delight in isolated particularity—in order to use all the resources of literary art to deal directly with the feeling of uncertainty, without falsely labelling it. Art is separated from life so that it may the more truthfully confront its anxieties. Coleridge, in the first version of 'Dejection' known as the 'Verses to Sara', does not even attempt such a transformation. The verse letter implicitly denies any distinction between the language of poetry and that of personal communication.

Wordsworth, in the first three months of 1802, seems to have tried repeatedly to reconcile his desire to speak to his own situation with a conviction that poetry is, first of all, a made thing, a constructed medium for a vision wherein the poet transforms his own concerns into another language before he expresses them. One of the poet's greatest resources, then, is his ability to exclude from the language of the poem the motives that may have made the poem necessary in the first place. Though the man that suffers may dwell at the centre of the mind that creates, and all the evidence suggests that it did for Wordsworth then, nevertheless the language of creation, the shadowy interposition, the tender fiction need not name its actual sources as long as it conveys their urgency. To be Home at Grasmere may have been unsatisfactory in many ways, ambitions may have been unrealized, but the language of the poetry need not suffer because of it.

However, all of Coleridge's literary activity during the same months seems to have been leading him, in spite of himself, in the other direction. However much he may have honoured the poet as maker, Coleridge seemed to be discovering that separating the making from the saying was impossible for him.

CHAPTER III

Toward Dejection

'THE POET is dead in me', wrote Coleridge to William Godwin in March 1801—just over a year before he composed the verse letter to Sara Hutchinson that became 'Dejection: an Ode'. 'My imagination (or rather the Somewhat that had been imaginative) lies, like a Cold Snuff on the circular Rim of a Brass Candle-stick, without even a stink of Tallow to remind you that it was once cloathed & mitred with Flame.' The letter was written at the end of three months of 'intellectual *exsiccation*', and equally severe physical illness (Wordsworth was to say in July that Coleridge had spent half of the previous ten months in bed). Specific names for Coleridge's illness may be unreliable (Wordsworth called it rheumatic fever), but Coleridge makes its symptoms all too explicit: 'a most excruciating pain on the least motion', 'my left Testicle swelled', 'pains in the calves of my legs' (January). And in spite of his claim of 'an almost compleat Recovery' in February, his health obviously continued to preoccupy him during March.

The letter to Godwin, Coleridge's notebook makes clear, was written during a day in bed when 'Wordsworth came—I talked with him—he left me alone—I shut my eyes' (*NB*, 925). The conversation must have been, for Coleridge, a depressing one: 'If I die' (he tells Godwin), 'and the Booksellers will give you any thing for my Life, be sure to say—"Wordsworth descended on him, like the Γνῶθι σεαυτον from Heaven; by shewing him what true Poetry was, he made him know, that he himself was no Poet."' And in a notebook entry for the next day, March 26th, Coleridge derives from Bartram's *Travels* 'a fantastic analogue & similitude to Wordsworth's Mind' that expresses in botanical terms the superiority of Wordsworth's fertile creativity: 'The soil is a deep, rich, dark Mould on a deep Stratum of tenacious Clay, and that on a foundation of Rocks, which often break through both Strata, lifting their back above the Surface. The Trees, which chiefly grow here, are the gigantic Black Oak, Magnolia, Fraxinus excelsior, Platane, & a few stately Tulip Trees' (*NB*, 926).

Although any single expression of doubt and self-questioning can always be ascribed to Coleridge's hypochondria, his penchant for self-pity, or his calculated design on the sympathy of his correspondent, together his complaints form a pattern of despair that was at least as real to the Wordsworths as to Coleridge himself. Apparently Dorothy Wordsworth sent her brother John an account of this visit of William to Keswick, for John replies to her (on March 29th) that 'You have made me quite melancholy this morning about Coleridge—I fear he will have had very bad health & it grieves me to think that he should be throwing himself away.' And Wordsworth himself, who may have gone to Keswick on March 25th to tell Coleridge that he was assuming the debt for the £30 that Longman had advanced to Coleridge, wrote two days later to Longman assuming the debt and encouraged Coleridge to add to this letter one of his own, in which Coleridge expressed to Longman his relief, his gratitude for the publisher's 'uniform delicacy, & liberality', and his own 'extreme Disgust which I feel at every perusal of my own Productions'. However, Coleridge's disgust was not quite complete; in the same letter he proposes that Longman publish an illustrated edition of the as yet uncompleted *Christabel*, with 'two Discourses, Concerning Metre, & Concerning the Marvelous in Poetry'. And indeed the despondent letter to Godwin had ended with a postscript inquiring what price 'an Author of reputation [might] fairly ask from a Bookseller for one Edition, of a 1000 Copies, of a five Shilling Book'.

Even allowing for the deceptive perplexities of Coleridge's situation in the spring of 1801, it is clear that his statement that the 'Poet is dead in me' is a gesture of despair pointing toward every aspect of his life. Health, money, friendship, creative composition, intellectual and metaphysical research, the weather, even the economic condition of the North of England are merged into a confusing mass of perceptions and frustrations, within which it is as impossible for Coleridge as for the reader to sort out cause from effect. He has begun obsessively to plan his emigration to a world that is physically and economically healthier but he has as yet no definite direction or destination. Two days before the letter to Godwin he wrote to Thomas Poole of his determination to find a land where external circumstance does not limit free activity, and although Coleridge denies that his expectation is dependent on 'any romantic Scheme' his tone echoes the idealistic enthusiasm of Pantisocracy of seven years before. Even the location has persisted: 'I would go and settle with Priestley in America . . . I say, I would go to America, if Wordsworth would go with me, & we could persuade two or three Farmers of this Country who are exceedingly attached to us—to accompany us.' At first emigration seems to represent an opportunity for realizing the full potentialities of the self: '*O for a lodge* in a Land where human Life was an end, to which Labor was only a Means, instead of being, as it [is] here, a mere means of carrying on Labor.' But then emigration becomes an escape from the visible manifestations of poverty: 'it is a matter of the utmost Importance to be removed from seeing and suffering *Want*.' Although Coleridge, in a letter next day to Poole, blames all this concern on his own hypochondria, 'a Rheumatism in the back part of my head', and the necessity of earning money by journalism, and although he insists that '. . . my Country is my country, and I will never leave it, till I am starved out of it', the project was to recur during the spring and summer in a variety of more insistent forms. The prospect of Coleridge living in the Azores was taken quite seriously by the Wordsworths from April until July, and even John Wordsworth (who stolidly argued that 'for an Englishman no place is equal to England') assisted in making specific arrangements.

But Coleridge's ill health and depressed circumstances can account for only part of the despondency with which he expresses his distrust of his future as a poet. The conclusion that the poet in him was dead seems also to have been the result of his own intellectual convictions, his radical questioning of the possible modes of knowledge, and his final distrust of the validity and possibility of poetry for a sensibility that operated as his did. For several months Coleridge had been actively concerned, as far as his health permitted him, in exploring pragmatically the ways of knowing. Early in February he disclosed to Humphry Davy a plan by which Wordsworth would rent Windy Brow from William Calvert so that Coleridge, William and Dorothy, and Calvert could set up there a laboratory for the study of chemistry. In explaining to Davy the reasons for Wordsworth's interest in such a project, Coleridge undoubtedly reveals his own as well: 'he feels it more & more necessary for him to have some intellectual pursuit less closely connected with deep passion, than Poetry.'

This relation of the intellect to the feelings, or 'the affinities of the Feelings with Words and Ideas', continues to perplex Coleridge throughout the spring of 1801. In a letter to Poole on March 23rd he attacks Newton as the exponent of the passive mind—'A lazy looker-on on an external World' whose system implicitly denies that the mind is 'made in God's Image, & that too in the sublimest sense—the Image of the *Creator*'. Yet he puts an inordinate amount of energy into speculations about the possibility of malting acorns, and in the letter to Longman described above he refers to 'the very important Researches & Studies, in which I have been lately immersed, & which have made all subjects of ordinary Interest [the context makes clear that this refers to his own poetry] appear to me *trifling* beyond measure'. It is too easy to resolve the paradox implied in Coleridge's attitude toward the creative superiority of the poet and the impersonal freedom of the scientist by calling it an ambivalence born of the fear of failure. Poetic composition puts him, as it does not Wordsworth, in a state of passive subjection to his own moods. In the letter to Godwin he complains that for him intense concentration on natural objects (without the discipline of science) leads inevitably to their disappearance into abstractions: 'I look at the Mountains only for the Curves of their outlines; the Stars, as I behold them, form themselves into Triangles.' In fact, these are the symptoms he describes of his 'intellectual *exsiccation*', the reasons for his conclusion that the poet in him is dead. And his notebook account of this passive subjection to the process of abstraction is more specific, and more revealing. After Wordsworth left him on March 25th, he lay in bed and 'I shut my eyes—beauteous spectra of two colors, orange and violet—then of green, which immediately changed to Peagreen, & then actually *grew* to my eye into a beautiful moss, the same as is on the mantle-piece at Grasmere.—abstract Ideas— & unconscious Links!!' (*NB*, 925). For Coleridge the problem lies not in the emptiness of abstraction, but in its vulnerability to uncontrolled associations—a problem that the verse letter to Sara Hutchinson a year later will dramatize.

A notebook entry slightly earlier also attempts to account for this process. Explicating the lines from 'Tintern Abbey' about seeing into the Life of Things, Coleridge explains:

By deep feeling we make our *Ideas dim*— & this is what we mean by our Life—ourselves. I think of the Wall—it is before me, a distinct Image—here. I necessarily think of the *Idea* & the Thinking I as two distinct & opposite Things. Now [let me] think of *myself*—of the thinking Being—the Idea becomes dim whatever it be—so dim that I know not what it is—but the Feeling is deep & steady—and this I call *I*—identifying the Percipient & the Perceived (*NB*, 921).

Thus through introspection and the accession of self-consciousness the sensation of colour (in the previous example) becomes moss collected for the mantel at Town End, but the imagined moss and all the associations of its location are parts of the poet's own being, for in the moment the percipient and perceived are identical. In being dependent upon the percipient's feeling, the perception gains its life. But that life is also created at the cost of the percipient's sense of a separable identity. Like a modern structuralist, Coleridge discovers that the subject cannot be an object, if it is an activity rather than a thing. And as for a structuralist, the discovery is enough to make him call all the humanistic heritage in doubt. 'We receive but what we give / And in our life alone does nature live', as Coleridge will write ambiguously to Sara Hutchinson a year later. Whether things spontaneously turn themselves into forms, or forms give birth to things, the situation Coleridge describes is one in which the perceiver lacks the control that, presumably, the successful poet must exert over his sensations. With intense sympathy Coleridge watches the four-year-old

Hartley try 'almost with convulsive Effort' to express the difference between the mountains he sees outside the window and the image of those mountains as they appear in a looking glass that his father holds over his head (*NB*, 923).

   Control, as much as sensitivity, is the essence of poetic genius that Coleridge finds lacking in himself, as he makes clear by two notebook entries later in that same spring. In one, in April, he copies with evident approval all of Giordano Bruno's 'sublime ode' about 'we [who] have known the Gift of Genius',

> And gaze undaunted on our shadowy fate
> Lest, being blind to light of the sun, or deaf
> To Nature's universal voices, we
> Receive the gifts of God ungraciously.
>
> We do not care at what low price fools rate us
> Nor mind how mad we look in the eyes of the world.
> We soar on stronger wings: we penetrate
> Beyond the cloudy pathways of the winds
> By power of vision—that is enough for us.
>
> ★   ★   ★
>
> Wings are not for mortals. Let the sun
> Go naked, unadorned by any cloud.
> Vision of truth! Quested, found, revealed,
> Take me—though more may follow where I go.
> If I am wise with Nature by God's bounty
> That is enough indeed, more than enough.

                    (*NB*, 929—translated by George Whalley)

It is, of course, impossible to know whether this statement of exultant confidence and power—we gaze undaunted, we soar, we penetrate—was copied out during one of those moments of temporary recovery of which Coleridge's letters (and the Wordsworths') speak, or whether Coleridge was again paying tribute, as he does in his remarks about Wordsworth, to a mode of genius diametrically opposed to his own. But the mood in Bruno's ode must be set against the words that Coleridge did directly apply to himself in a notebook entry of about the same date. 'Mind, shipwrecked by storms of doubt, now masterless, rudderless, shattered, —pulling in the dead swell of a dark & windless Sea' (*NB*, 932).

In the weeks that followed, Coleridge's expressions of defeat became increasingly morbid, the scheme for escaping to the Azores more definite and more desperate. To George Greenough he writes, on April 13th,

I feel that I 'to the grave go down.'—As a Husband, & a Father, as a young Man who had dar'd hope that he, even he, might sometime benefit his fellow creatures, I wish to live, but I have kept my *best* hope so unprofan'd by Ambition, so pure from the love of Praise, & I have so deep an intuition that *to cease to be* are sounds without meaning, that though I wish to live, yet the Thought of Death is never for a moment accompanied by Gloom, much less terror, in my feelings or imagination.

The metaphor of sinking into the grave pervades the correspondence of the spring: to Poole on April 18th: 'I feel and am certain, that "I to the Grave go down".', to Thelwall on April 23rd: '. . . Indeed, I feel & know, that (at all event if I stay in this climate) I am going down to the Grave. . . .' On May 4th to Davy, the metaphor has almost yielded to hysteria: '*Sinking, sinking, sinking!* I feel, that I am *sinking!* . . . I am at times an object of moral Disgust to my own Mind.'

Perhaps it is impossible to locate anything like a direct cause for despondency such as this. To blame it on the frustrations of his life with Sara Coleridge and the hopelessness of his love for Sara Hutchinson is to adopt assumptions about human motivation too simple at least for Coleridge. Domestic misery, disease, a crisis in personal convictions, jealousy of Wordsworth all contribute. But the effect, for the literary biographer, is obviously more important than the cause, especially when the effect seems to be an eager desire to escape from imaginative activity either by moving to the Azores or by finding something impersonal to write. He never suggests that the Azores project, which he says he does not like to think about when he is well, is anything more than expedient, and it is not clear how seriously he took the project. Though he tells Humphry Davy in May that William and Dorothy will go with him, he also pleads for Davy's silence, 'for the scheme . . . is rather the Thing of a *Wish* than of a *Hope*'. Neither William nor Dorothy

ever seems to have taken their own part in the project very
seriously, but John Wordsworth wrote at least one solemn, well-
meaning letter of advice (to Dorothy) about Coleridge's plan—'of
this I am certain that it would be very imprudent in Colridge to
take Mrs Col: with him till he has seen the place'—and the methods
of obtaining passage. Apparently accepting the Wordsworths'
reluctance to join him, he asks Davy (in May) whether T. R.
Underwood would like to accompany him, and in July tells
Poole that he had postponed and hoped to relinquish the Azores
plan altogether until another attack—this time of nausea and
giddiness—forced him to reconsider it. Decision now, by mid-
summer, seemed to be imperative, and impossible. 'Something I
must do, & that speedily—for Body & Soul are going—Soul is
going into Body, and Body is going into Dung & Crepitus—
with more of the latter than the former.'

But the Azores project, however closely dependent on his
physical condition, is also an alternative to literary composition.
The almost obsessive nature of the language used in the letters
suggests how thoroughly Coleridge's sense of his condition was
influenced by the metaphors through which he saw it, and how
urgently he sought some other literary form with which to
define himself. Health, money, emigration, imaginative composition are parallel terms for the condition from which he finds
himself alienated, terms which make cause and effect as impossible
for the reader to separate as for Coleridge. Language most suggestive of 'Dejection: an Ode' first appears a year before the poem
was begun, in the April 28th letter to Godwin:

... I am not dissembling when I express my exceeding scepticism
respecting the sanity of my own Feelings & Tone of Intellect, relatively
to a work of Sentiment & Imagination. I have been compelled ... to
seek resources in austerer reasonings— & have thereby so denaturalized
my mind, that I can scarcely convey to you the disgust with which I
look over any of my own compositions. ...

Journalism he regards as possible for the sake of income (in May
he wrote to Daniel Stuart requesting a list of subjects), but any
other form of writing is impossible. In June he tells Godwin,

O God! all but dear & lovely Things seemed to be known to my Imagination only as Words—even the Forms which struck terror into me in my fever dreams were still forms of Beauty.

If summer did not bring Coleridge either health or literary inspiration, it at least encouraged movement and intellectual activity, the further use of the resources of austerest reasonings. In July he left Keswick for the East Riding of Yorkshire—to read Duns Scotus (and Locke, Hume, Hobbes) at the Cathedral Library in Durham, and to visit Sara Hutchinson at Bishop Middleham and accompany her on a long visit to Gallow Hill. The month's absence from Keswick, the return of his brother-in-law Robert Southey from Portugal, the presence of Sara, must all have contributed to the more controlled, sometimes jolly, tone of the summer letters. In the jokes (about the Durham librarian who took a request for Leibniz to be one for Live Nits), in doggerel verse (to Isabella Anderson and Joanna Hutchinson), in his spirited defence to Godwin of Conversation Sharp and Samuel Rogers as summer visitors and literary pilgrims, even in the endlessly involved financial letters to Poole, appears a Coleridge who sometimes found wit and subtlety as replacements for self-pity. To be sure the schemes for emigration still abound (including this time a plan to visit Pinney's estate in St. Nevis or to accompany Thomas Wedgwood to Sicily), but Coleridge himself is conscious of a new mood: 'My spirits are good' he tells Poole early in September, '—I am generally *cheerful*, & when I am not, it is only because I have exchanged it for a deeper & more pleasurable Tranquillity.' Unlike a soldier, whose trade is 'to follow a blind feeling— & thereby to act', his trade has been 'to contemplate— & thereby to *endure*'.

Although Coleridge in the late summer was still afflicted by a variety of humiliating ailments (boils, a swollen knee, bilious colic), and although serious literary composition was as remote a resource as ever, the necessity for endurance, even escape, is now more directly ascribed to domestic dissatisfaction. Perhaps the time spent with Sara Hutchinson made Coleridge more sensitive to what Dorothy Wordsworth, for one, found Mrs. Coleridge's outstanding deficiency: 'her radical fault is want of sensibility, what can such a woman be to Coleridge?' He may hesitate to explain to Godwin (in September) the 'additional sources of Disquietude' that have plagued him because Godwin has not known him long enough to be interested in 'Carcase Coleridge', but the resolve does not last out the letter. If he comes to London to work for the *Morning Post*, he tells Godwin, 'I come *alone. Here* it will be imprudent for me to stay, from the wet & the cold— even if everything within doors were as well suited for my head & heart, as my head & heart would, I trust, be to everything that was wise & amiable.' In writing to his brother-in-law Southey he is, understandably, more blunt, and far more interesting. The plan now is that he will go to London in about two weeks (early in November), stay a few weeks, then visit Poole in Nether Stowey or the Wedgwoods in Dorset for the worst of the winter. Separation from Sara Coleridge is essential—for his tranquillity and for the recovery of his imagination.

October brought some consolations for Coleridge: the reunion with Wordsworth, now back from Scotland, celebrated in the 'Ode to Rain'; the extended visit at Keswick of Southey, who had returned from Portugal; the visits of Tom (and later Mary) Hutchinson. Dorothy Wordsworth's *Journal* does not make clear whether Coleridge's presence at Grasmere so often during the month was caused by very extensive visits or very frequent ones. On October 10th, Coleridge, Dorothy and William built Sara's Seat. On October 23rd, Coleridge notes the arrival of Mary Hutchinson, presumably at Keswick though she will spend the winter at Grasmere. The pages torn from Dorothy's *Journal* probably have removed forever the most interesting account of the days immediately preceding Coleridge's departure for London on November 10th, but the effect of that departure on Dorothy was intensely emotional. On November 9th, when the *Journal* resumes after the missing entries for the preceding five days, she, William and Mary walk from Grasmere to Keswick with him, and 'Mary and I sate in C's room a while'. The next afternoon, 'Poor C. left us' and during their return to Grasmere,

Every sight and every sound reminded me of him—dear, dear fellow, of his many walks to us by day and by night, of all dear things. I was

melancholy, and could not talk, but at last I eased my heart by weeping
—nervous blubbering, says William. It is not so. O! how many, many
reasons have I to be anxious for him.

Dorothy's remark about William's lack of sympathy—a rare
complaint in the *Journal*—suggests that Dorothy's pity is not
aroused just by the obvious facts of Coleridge's uncertain health or
future, but is complicated by her own antipathy to Mrs. Coleridge
and her anxiety about Coleridge's attachment to Sara Hutchinson.
The very pleasant days they have just spent at Keswick, for
instance, occurred when Mrs. Coleridge and the children were
apparently visiting the Clarksons at Eusemere (where Coleridge
stopped to bid them goodbye on his way to London). It is even
perhaps worth speculating that the missing pages of the *Journal*
give some account of domestic turmoil in the Coleridge household
that explain why Mrs. Coleridge and the children so suddenly
visit people who had been at Grasmere from October 28th to
November 5th, and why Coleridge arrived at Grasmere on the
day after the Clarksons must have stopped at Keswick on their
way home to Eusemere on the 5th.

Coleridge's letter to Southey just before leaving on November
9th, his letters to Southey later in the winter, his notebook
entries for December, suggest how intensely unpleasant the
domestic tone of these last few days at Keswick must have been.
Anticipating his farewell to wife and children the following day,
he tells Southey on November 9th: 'If my wife loved me, and I
my wife, half as well as we both love our children, I should be the
happiest man alive—but this is not—will not be.' Later, in December, his tone to Southey is more despondent.

Heaven knows that many & many & many a time I have regarded my
Talents & Acquirements as a Porter's Burthen, imposing on me the
Duty of going on to the end of the Journey, when I would gladly lie
down by the side of the road, & become the Country for a mighty
nation of Maggots—for what is Life, gangrened, as it is with me, and
in it's very vitals—domestic Tranquility?

Though the account he sent Wedgwood almost a year later, after
a promised 'amendment', refers to events after his return north in

the spring of 1802, some of its details must also apply to the household he was now leaving:

Ill tempered speeches sent after me when I went out of the House, ill-tempered Speeches on my return, my friends received with freezing looks, the least opposition or contradiction occasioning screams of passion, & the sentiments, which I held most base, ostentatiously avowed—all this added to the utter negation of all, which a Husband expects from a Wife—especially, living in retirement— & the consciousness, that I was myself growing a worse man O dear Sir! no one can tell what I have suffered.

Recently published letters of Southey confirm that this visit to London was primarily to be a separation from Sara Coleridge. Immediately after Coleridge arrived in London, Southey told Charles Danvers that the length of Coleridge's stay 'depends upon his inclination, and that is the most unsteady of all things'. But during the winter Coleridge must at some time have told his brother-in-law that he had intended to leave his wife permanently, for early in February Southey, writing again to Danvers, complains that 'After all his foolish gossiping about his wife [Coleridge] now talks about returning in six weeks to Keswick. . . .'[1]

In his domestic uncertainty Coleridge was beginning to discover literary possibilities. Although he still gave himself every excuse for not writing, from the unsuitability of his circumstances to the inferiority of his talent, sometime in December he rather ambitiously projected

a *Series* of love Poems—truly Sapphic, save that they shall have a large Interfusion of moral Sentiment & calm Imagery on Love in all the moods of the mind—Philosophic, fantastic, in moods of enthusiasm, of simple Feeling, of mysticism, of Religion—comprize in it all the practice, & all the philosophy of Love   (*NB*, 1064).

But the next entry in the notebook, presumably a précis for the first of the series, is presented in terms less abstract, terms that suggest the first step of the process of composing personal domestic chaos as literary form, and anticipate the verse letter to Sara Hutchinson, and its revision as 'Dejection: an Ode':

[1] *New Letters of Robert Southey*, edited by K. Curry (New York, 1965), I, 255, 271–2.

A lively picture of a man, disappointed in marriage, & endeavoring to make a compensation to himself by virtuous & tender & brotherly friendship with an amiable Woman—the obstacles—the jealousies—the impossibility of it—But advice that he should as much as possible withdraw himself from pursuits of morals &c— & devote himself to abstract sciences.

The modes of escape Coleridge chose—emotional, intellectual, geographic—seem to have been at first successful. When he arrived in London in mid-November he was apparently in better spirits than he had been for weeks. The first letter sent North seemed to Dorothy 'cheerful', and although a note from Mrs. Coleridge received at Grasmere on November 24th reports that he is 'very ill', his letter on November 30th reports that he is 'very well', and the ones received on December 4th from Sara Hutchinson and Coleridge are both 'written in good spirits'. From this distance, new hopes of a reunified sensibility occur to him. He tells his wife he has accepted with enthusiasm the invitation of Wedgwood to spend three months with him in Cornwall, because 'it is of the first importance to me to make the connection with the Wedgwoods one of Love & *personal* attachment, as well as of moral calculation & intellectual Hope—which are subject to sad Caprices in this mortal Life'. And the statement reminds him inexorably of his family: 'O my dear Hartley—my Derwent! my [children]!—The night before last I dreamt [I saw] them so vividly, that I was quite ill in the morning—& wept my eyes red —which was good for me.'

Although the details of Coleridge's days in London are not easy to discover, it is clear that they were busy: on November 19th, for instance, he was 'engaged in the City', then at Lamb's until seven; on the 20th he visited Godwin, and at some time during the next week he moved from Southey's where he had been staying temporarily, to live in King Street (Covent Garden) with a tailor named Howell. Although at that time he was still planning to leave London in ten days to spend three months with Wedgwood in Cornwall, he did not leave London until the day after Christmas—to visit Poole in Nether Stowey rather than Wedgwood in Cornwall, to stay three weeks not three months.

The London that Coleridge stayed in in the winter of 1801–2 was a busy, bustling, vulgar place—at least as the quality of its life is reflected in the pages of Daniel Stuart's *Morning Post*, for which Coleridge worked, and in the ecstatic account of it Lamb gives in his essay 'The Londoner', in the *Morning Post* for 1 February 1802. Although Kemble in *Richard III* was presented each Monday 'until further notice' at Drury Lane, and a 'New and Improved Edition of the Works of the Late Benjamin Franklin' had just been published, and frequent book auctions were held in King Street and elsewhere in Covent Garden, at the same time 'Mice are becoming scarce, in consequence of the great demand of their skin for ladies' eyebrows', a Mr. Dufour was advertising 'bougies and sexual remedies', and the classified columns are filled with countless advertisements for abortionists and homes for unmarried mothers. The Leicester Square Panorama offered views of Constantinople, and Uncle David begged his valued nephew, 'Before you come to Town, tell me, I beseech you, where I can WRITE to you?—'twill save you from a world of woe.' Obviously the vision of a tawdry hell that enlivens book VII of *The Prelude* was in full vigour (in fact William and Dorothy visited Bartholomew Fair with the Lambs later that year), but urban chaos never seems to have aroused either Coleridge's interest or his hatred. Of course none of his letters to the Wordsworths, or Sara Hutchinson, survive from this period, but the letters he sent to other people from London are never as interesting about the city as they ought to have been, or as Wordsworth's probably would have been. Even Southey's reports on the quality of London life this winter are more lively: 'This London', he tells John Rickman in February, 'poisons my body, and God knows it is not the most favorable atmosphere for my brain. ... Carriages driven by Steam are the most important novelties.' The city for Coleridge, however, was not a culture, nor as yet a form of the cold inanimate world. It was simply a succession of people.

Correspondence between London and Grasmere that winter was frequent and intense, as the records of it in Dorothy's *Journal* indicate. And there were important things to write about: by December William had begun writing poetry again, Annette had been heard from, probably William's intention to marry Mary Hutchinson had been disclosed to Coleridge. On December 18th Dorothy 'wrote to Coleridge for money', and on the 21st William wrote to Daniel Stuart asking to borrow £10 that Coleridge had 'neglected' to give him but that he now needs for a 'particular occasion'.

Stuart and Coleridge later disagreed about the importance of Coleridge's contributions to the *Morning Post*. Stuart, in self defence, tried to deny their importance in order to justify his failure to have paid Coleridge more generously for them, just as Coleridge exaggerated their importance in order to justify his failure to write anything more than journalism. But as Stuart recalled years later, Coleridge's career as a working, day-to-day journalist had been something less than a success in 1800 and it is unlikely to have been more successful during this winter:

My practice was to call on him in the middle of the day, talk over the news, and project a leading paragraph for the next morning. In conversation he would make a brilliant display. . . . Having arranged with him the matter of a leading paragraph one day, I went about six o'clock for it; I found him stretched on the sofa groaning with pain. He had not written a word; nor could he write. The subject was one of a temporary, an important, and a pressing nature. I returned to the Morning Post Office, wrote it out myself, and then I went to Coleridge at Howell's, read it over, begged he would correct it, and decorate it a little with some of his graceful touches. When I had done reading, he exclaimed, "Me correct that: It is as well written as I or any other man could write it." And so I was obliged to content myself with my own works.[1]

In fact Lamb, explaining to John Rickman in February 1802 his own resignation from the *Morning Post*, blames it partly on Coleridge:

. . . Stuart was wonderfully polite and civil at first, I suppose because Coleridge recommended me, from whose assistance in the Paper he expected great things, but Coleridge from ill health and unsettlement having hung an Arse, as the saying is, I gradually got out of favor. . . .

[1] *Gentleman's Magazine*, May-June 1838 (2, IX, 485, 577).

Assuming that Coleridge's connection with the *Morning Post* that winter was almost as tenuous as Stuart says it had been earlier, it is all the more difficult to discover the economy of his energies. Though Southey and Coleridge arrived in London at about the same time, and Coleridge spent his first week at Southey's lodgings in Bridge Street, they seem to have had little to do with one another subsequently. Southey told Charles Danvers in December that 'I see him but seldom. His dislike to London is only when he is obliged to work in it, or when he is away; otherwise he certainly likes the perpetual stimulation of company, which he cannot procure elsewhere.' Although a month earlier Southey had urged John Rickman to change his subscription from the *Star* to the *Morning Post* 'in which you will see good things from [Coleridge]', there is no mention at all of any specific writing. He tells of Coleridge's imminent visit to the Wedgwoods and his talking of 'returning to pass some months in London', but gives no other indication of Coleridge's activities. As Coleridge later told Sotheby, he had been reading Plato (*Parmenides* and *Timaeus*) for his 'curious metaphysical work' during the winter; and he obviously visited Lamb and Godwin occasionally (though not frequently enough to please Godwin). Living close to both Royal theatres, Covent Garden and Drury Lane, he had the opportunity to see Kemble in *Hamlet* and *Richard III*, *Macbeth*, *The Merchant of Venice*, *Henry V*, *Othello* and *The School for Scandal*.

Perhaps it is indicative of Coleridge's attitude toward the public world and the *Morning Post* in particular that his most significant contribution to the paper that winter was not one of his political essays, whose interest barely survives their topicality, but his 'Ode to Tranquillity', published on December 4th. On its first appearance the poem had two prefatory stanzas, later discarded, dismissing the very subjects of his own political essays and celebrating the virtues of a retired life. The problems of half-thinking, sensual France—a natural slave—disturb him not, and even the subjugation of Switzerland occasions only a few tears. Such events, and the crude treaties they produced, are merely the green fuel, he says, which seasoned by time will feed the funeral pyre of nations, in some future Armageddon. The only sane pose, he argues, is a sort of quietism and indifference, not sloth or satiety, but a willed freedom from the bubble of Idle Hope and the spectre of dire Remembrance,

> . . . while within myself I trace
> The greatness of some unborn race,
> Aloof with Hermit Eye I scan
> The present works of present man
> A wild and dreamlike Trade of Blood & Guile,
> Too foolish for a Tear, too wicked for a Smile![1]

The one positive image of tranquillity, appropriately, is a recollection of the day in Grasmere the previous autumn when he helped 'in the sultry summer's heat' to build a 'mossy seat', and in the text of the poem that Sara Hutchinson put into her collection of *Sara's Poets* the following spring, the pronouns for Tranquillity are ambiguous enough so that the poem with few alterations becomes a love poem to her.

The Christmas trip to Stowey, anticipated months in advance but suddenly prompted by a letter received on Christmas day, did not bring the healthful recuperation he had expected. Having for ten days of the three weeks suffered from nightly bowel attacks, he cancelled the projected visit to his family at Ottery St. Mary, and returned to London on January 21st. While he was at Stowey he had the companionship of both Poole and Wedgwood, but it seems unlikely that the connection with the Wedgwoods could have become, as he had dreamed, 'one of Love & *personal* attachment, as well as of moral calculation & intellectual Hope' under those conditions.

Perhaps because Coleridge's health had improved enough to allow him to be more active, or perhaps merely because the letters surviving after his return to London are more frequent and more interesting, the impression is that his second six-week residence in the city was far more productive. The morning he left for Stowey he had breakfasted with his Bristol friend Humphry Davy, and his return on the 21st was apparently planned to coincide with the opening of Davy's lectures at the Royal

[1] The text used here is that of *Sara's Poets* (see note to p. 7) above), as reprinted in George Whalley's *Coleridge and Sara Hutchinson*.

Institution. Davy's astonishing success in these lectures, after what his biographer calls 'various mortifications', was one of the most impressive social and intellectual events of the London season. The twenty-two-year-old man, whom Coleridge had known since Davy was at nineteen the director of the Pneumatic Institute at Bristol, had been invited in January 1801 to give a series of lectures at the Royal Institution, with the understanding that he would soon become its sole professor of chemistry. Count Rumford, when he met Davy in March, apparently regretted the extravagance of his promises, but the 'mortifications' were short-lived. Rumford, hearing him lecture, said 'Let him command any arrangements which the Institution can afford'; a few weeks later Davy was elected to the Trepidarian Society ('which consisted of twenty-five of the most violent republicans of the day'), by June he was made Lecturer, in July he was given three months leave of absence to study the tanning industry in the west of England. At some time during the year he found time to write a rather substantial ode to 'The Power of the Eternal Cause informing Natural Phenomena'.

The introductory lecture which Coleridge returned to London to attend on January 25th was an eloquent, enthusiastic appeal for the recognition of the role of science in a dynamic and progressive society, and in the intellectual life of a modern educated man. Beginning with the argument that chemistry is the essential science, more fundamental than but related to all the others, contributing to the useful arts of industry and agriculture, Davy went on to argue that the pursuit of science is highly beneficial to the individual mind and an act of civilization on the part of society as a whole. Because of the proliferation of knowledge through printing, the increasing dependence of one area of society on another, and the greater attentiveness to 'the realities of life' on the part of the 'rich and privileged orders', Davy looks forward to 'a bright day of which we already behold the dawn'. The study of experimental chemistry in particular, even by an amateur, enables an individual to gain 'a permanent and placid enjoyment' in the 'contemplation of the various phenomena of the external world'. Surely Coleridge must have felt he was being offered an alternative both to the fevered but passive existence of his own emotional life and to the quietism of tranquillity. The study of chemistry Davy offered as a means of self-control and general understanding.

The objects that are nearest to man are the first to occupy his attention: from considering their agencies on each other he becomes capable of predicting effects; in modifying these effects he gains activity; and science becomes the parent of the strength and independence of his faculties. . . . In common society, to men collected in great cities, who are wearied by the constant recurrence of similar artificial pursuits and objects, and who are in need of sources of permanent attachment, the cultivation of chemistry and the physical sciences may be eminently beneficial. . . . It may destroy diseases of the imagination, owing to too deep a sensibility; and it may attach the affections to objects, permanent, important, and intimately related to the interests of the human species. Even to persons of powerful minds, who are connected with society by literary, political, or moral relations, an acquaintance with the science that represents the operations of nature cannot be wholly useless. It must strengthen their habits of minute discrimination; and by obliging them to use a language representing simple facts, may tend to destroy the influence of terms connected only with feeling. The man who has been accustomed to study natural objects philosophically, to be perpetually guarding against the delusions of the fancy, will not readily be induced to multiply words so as to forget things. . . . Perceiving in all the phenomena of the universe the designs of a perfect intelligence, he will be averse to the turbulence and passion of hasty innovations, and will uniformly appear as the friend of tranquillity and order

(*Works* (London, 1839), II, 325–6).

These concluding sentences of Davy's first lecture must have been more than familiar to Coleridge, for they undoubtedly continue a discussion he and Davy had been conducting since Coleridge had written to him a year before asking advice for setting up a chem-istry laboratory for himself and the Wordsworths. And of course the argument for chemical experimentation as therapy, both for the philosopher inclined to be too abstruse and the lover too attached by passion, had appeared in Coleridge's notebooks and letters for the last year. 'Multiplying words so as to forget things' was a vice that Coleridge was as eager to admit as others were to ascribe to him, and he repeatedly saw himself as unable to attain that balance between submission to events and appetite that Davy calls the state of nature, and the abstruse submission to words that Davy calls a disease of the imagination. But Davy's plea for the benefits of chemical study perhaps explains Coleridge's continued presence at the series of lectures, and his notes of them, more satisfactorily than does his later comment that he went seeking metaphors for poetry.

Coleridge's lecture notes too tend to discredit his explanation that he sought metaphors. If, as Davy's biographer Paris suggests, the unorthodox style of Davy's lectures shocked those who believed in the purity of scientific discourse, none of this impurity appears in Coleridge's notebook. Aside from a few jokes about the potential usefulness of explosive gases for destroying the aristocrats in the audience, the notes are straightforward accounts of the experiments Davy used to illustrate the lectures. Only in one retrospective note does he allude to the occasion on January 28th when Davy 'gave a spark with the Electric machine—I felt nothing —he gave a very vivid spark with the Leyden Phial— & I distinctly felt the shock' (*NB*, 1099). The experience was apparently recorded as an instance of 'Strength of Feeling connected with vividness of Idea'. In one of the essays 'On Method' in the *Friend*, Coleridge more extensively described his debt to Davy, and to the chemist's discipline where 'the serious complacency which is afforded by the sense of truth, utility, permanence, and progression, blends with and ennobles the exhilarating surprise and pleasurable sting of curiosity' (*Friend*, Section II, vi). It is no less than poetry realized in nature, the corollary of Shakespeare's ability to realize nature in poetry. But at the time of the lectures, Coleridge must have felt he was being offered a respectable alternative to the uncertainties of the poet's dependence on the creations of his own mind.

If Davy's general argument for the historical and sociological importance of science was familiar to Coleridge (indeed it almost echoes Wordsworth's comments on the man of science in the 1801 preface to the second edition of *Lyrical Ballads* and anticipates the language of the 1815 supplementary essay), to the rest of Davy's audience the lecture was fresh and exhilarating. A contemporary account by Purkis says the sensation and admiration were 'scarcely to be imagined':

Men of the first rank and talent—the literary and the scientific, the practical and the theoretical, blue-stockings, and women of fashion, the old and the young, all crowded—eagerly crowded the lecture-room. His youth, his simplicity, his natural eloquence, his chemical knowledge, his happy illustrations and well-conducted experiments, excited universal attention and unbounded applause. Compliments, invitations, and presents, were showered upon him in abundance from all quarters; his society was courted by all, and all appeared proud of his acquaintance.[1]

And Davy's biographer Paris is hardly more restrained than Davy's friend Purkis:

... behold him in the Theatre of the Royal Institution, surrounded by an aristocracy of intellect as well as of rank; by the flowers of genius, the *élite* of fashion, and the beauty of England, whose very respirations were suspended in eager expectation to catch his novel and satisfactory elucidations of the mysteries of Nature (Paris, I, 136).

Although Coleridge appears to have avoided the Masquerade at Ranelagh that followed the Trepidarians' supper celebrating the first lecture, much of his intense social activity during January and February was undoubtedly part of his share in Davy's triumph. In the letter to his wife on February 24th, Coleridge with playful exaggeration describes the kind of success that he 'could' have as a '*tonish*' poet, the kind obviously that Davy was enjoying as a tonish chemist:

I assure you, I am quite a man of *fashion*—so many titled acquaintances — & handsome Carriages stopping at my door— & fine *Cards*—and then I am such an exquisite Judge of Music, & Painting— & pass criticisms on furniture & chandeliers— & pay such very handsome Compliments to all Women of Fashion/that I do verily believe, that if I were to stay 3 months in town & have tolerable health & spirits, I should be a Thing in Vogue—the very *tonish* Poet & Jemmy Jessamy fine Talker in Town. If you were only to see the tender Smiles that I

[1] Quoted by J. A. Paris, *Life of Sir Humphry Davy* (London, 1831), I, 134–5.

occasionally receive from the Honorable Mrs Damer—you would scratch her eyes out, for Jealousy. And then there's the *sweet* (N.B. musky) Lady Charlotte — nay but I won't tell you her name you might perhaps take it into yr head to write an Anonymous Letter to her, & disturb our little innocent amour.—

Mocking himself as the country poet among exquisite chandeliers and musky ladies is the kind of game Coleridge rarely indulged in —or knew well enough to play successfully. The example of Davy being courted by Duchesses must have suggested that anything was possible in his world, but Coleridge was nevertheless still eager to escape from it: 'O that I were at Keswick with my Darlings! My Hartley / My fat Derwent!' Davy's success, it is clear, antagonized Southey as much as it amused Coleridge. The 'silent estrangement' that came between them Southey blamed on Davy's success, on the diverging of their interests and habits of life, thinking, study. And their relationship, unlike that between Davy and Coleridge, is free of metaphysics, that unifying interest that is also, to Southey, 'a foul weed that poisons whatever it clings to'.[1]

   The work that was going forward—against ill health, against the fussing recriminations of Godwin, against the memories of 'the heart-withering Conviction—that I could not be happy without my children, & could not but be miserable with the mother of them', against the resistible temptation to join Davy's high life — was a 'great metaphysical book' on time and space to be produced by Thomas Wedgwood and James Mackintosh with a 'preface on the history of metaphysical speculations' by Coleridge. As Southey feared, the book (which had begun in the correspondence with Josiah Wedgwood the previous winter and spring) did prove an abortion rather than a birth.
   And in spite of the distractions in the life of a London journalist and friend of the great, Coleridge was still obsessed with the impossibility, yet necessity, of literary composition. In the midst of defending himself against Godwin's accusation that he had been indifferent to and neglectful of him, Coleridge goes on

[1] Letter to Charles Danvers, 2 December 1801, in *New Letters*, I, 261.

to explain that if he has been harsh and unfeeling toward Godwin, it is not vanity but its absence that has motivated his neglect:

As an *Author*, at all events, I have neither Vanity nor ambition—I think meanly, of all that I have done, and if ever I hope proudly of my future Self, this Hot Fit is uniformly followed & punished by Languor, & Despondency—or rather, by lazy & unhoping Indifference (22 January 1802).

Whether or not he felt he had discovered anything, Coleridge's return to Keswick at the beginning of March was to be, he hoped, the inauguration of a new and more tranquil period in his life. To his wife he writes on February 19th that '. . . it is my frequent prayer, & my almost perpetual aspiration, that we may meet to part no more— & live together as affectionate Husband & Wife ought to do'. But much of the amendment anticipated—in health, in domestic circumstance, in literary activity—is again dependent on a scheme for emigration. This time he hopes for 'a two year's residence at Montpelier—under blue skies & in a rainless air' with Southey's company for 'some months'. Less than a week later the plan has become far more elaborate, even fantastic: 'Wordsworth will marry soon after my return [to Keswick in March]; & he, Mary, & Dorothy will be our companions & neighbours. . . . About July we shall all [including Southey] set sail from Liverpool to Bordeaux.' Even his regular correspondence with the Words-worths, who must have expressed some misgivings about the scheme or at least qualified their willingness to join it, does not seem to have dampened his enthusiasm.

If from London everything seemed possible, Coleridge must have incurred some checks to his optimism during his trip to Keswick by way of Gallow Hill at the end of February. His intention to accompany Sara Hutchinson from Gallow Hill to Grasmere, so that she can be with Mary until the wedding, was disappointed. He stopped with Tom Hutchinson and his sister from March 2nd until March 13th, but then went on alone 'in a violent storm of snow & Wind' to Scotch Corner and Keswick. What happened during his eleven days with Sara at Gallow Hill can only be imagined—though the intense tone of those days is suggested by some of the fragmentary notations Coleridge made during them:

Wordsworth & [?M]—S & Coler.—Little Boy seeking me—N.B. poems—(*NB*, 1144)

And later:

Gallow Hill, Thursday, March 11th, 1802
S. T. Coleridge
Sara
 SarHa
 Friday, March 12th/' & wept aloud'—you made me feel uncomfortable (*NB*, 1150, 1151).

Geoffrey Yarlott finds in these notes a paradigm for Coleridge's predicament: the irreconcilable obligations produced by his love for Sara Hutchinson and his duties as a father, especially to Hartley.[1]

When Coleridge actually arrived at Keswick is unclear. The projected visit to Strutt at Derby was apparently cancelled, because he obviously did not stop, at least for any length of time, on his way to Gallow Hill, and it would have been far out of his way to go there on his way from Gallow Hill to Keswick. Though the first visit to Grasmere recorded in Dorothy's *Journal* is that of March 19th, it is clear that he must have been at Keswick at least part of the previous five days, and probably Wordsworth went to Keswick on the 18th to bring him next day to Grasmere. The last letter from Coleridge that Dorothy records is the one that arrived on March 6th, while Coleridge was still at Gallow Hill, and Dorothy last mentions writing to him at Gallow Hill on March 8th.

Wherever and whenever the first meeting in four months between Coleridge and the Wordsworths took place, it was the occasion of the first of many talks far into the night. Now for the first time Coleridge had to express frankly his hopes for the amendment of his domestic life, hopes perhaps compromised by his stay at Gallow Hill on the way home, and to urge again his

[1] Geoffrey Yarlott, *Coleridge and the Abyssinian Maid*, pp. 246-7.

scheme for emigration and hear the misgivings of William and Dorothy. And this must have been the occasion on which William first told Coleridge of the postponement of his marriage to Mary, and the possibility of his meeting Annette at Calais in September. Both questions, Dorothy reports, were 'resolved' on March 22nd.

It is not surprising that their first literary conversations should have concerned writers such as Ben Jonson, rather than themselves. Neither poet had finished a substantial work during the four months of their separation. To be sure, after tea on Saturday (the 20th) William read 'The Pedlar' to Dorothy and Coleridge, but the revisions can hardly have made an enormous impact on Coleridge, who had been listening to versions of the poem for almost four years. Far more affecting, to Coleridge, must have been the twice postponed return visit of the Wordsworths to Keswick, which finally occurred on March 28th, the day after 'Wm wrote part of an ode', two days after he wrote 'The Rainbow' while Dorothy was getting into bed. It may be frivolous to suggest that had they gone to Keswick when they planned, or even on the second date they set, Wordsworth never would have written either poem, but on such tenuous events the history of literature must always depend.

At some moment between their arrival 'wet to the skin' on Sunday the 28th and the following Sunday, April 4th, William obviously read to Coleridge whatever of the Ode he had finished. The week was full of activities that left little time for poetry reading—William and Coleridge to Armathwaite on Monday, to the Calverts on Tuesday, Portinscale on Wednesday (Calverts and Williamsons at dinner), to 'the How' and Portinscale again on Thursday, to Skiddaw on Saturday (dinner at the Calverts)—and probably Coleridge did not hear the new poems until Dorothy read them on Sunday after dinner. But whenever Coleridge first heard the Ode, the effect must have been in some way over-whelming. He did not find himself in prayer, as he said he did after hearing *The Prelude* (in 'To William Wordsworth'), but writing to Sara Hutchinson a letter in verse that perhaps of all that Coleridge ever wrote most clearly illustrates his achievements and weaknesses as a man and as a writer. It was an assembling of lines, perhaps ostensibly in answer to the letter from Sara that arrived on Monday, into which more than a year of suffering and frustration had gone.

It hardly needs to be said that the verse letter to Sara has no real subject other than its composer, that its addressee is often more a convenience than a loved one oramuse. In succeeding months Coleridge not only addressed one version of it to Wordsworth, he even told Thomas Poole (in May) that it had been written originally to him. Like Wordsworth's Ode and 'Resolution and Independence' the poem belongs to the vague category of the spring elegy, a complaint about emotional dearth existing in the midst of and in spite of the natural vitality of the season. But even this convention, for Coleridge, is more an excuse than an occasion. Only Coleridge could have written a poem like this, and it is almost as clear that he could hardly have written it, or wanted to write it, at any other moment in his career. He succeeds in doing, profusely, exactly what Wordsworth was trying to avoid: to expose the subjective language of the self.

Except for meteorological conditions (the crescent moon waning, the inconstant wind, the depressed atmosphere), nothing in the poem is finite. And it is to the oddness of the weather that Coleridge constantly returns, in anxiety and expectation, seeking some sort of reaffirmation. Once scene and lament succumb to the poet's cry of despair and need, the poem simply becomes the poet—he and it together greedily consume all distinctions, annihilate all control. No poem could more directly contravene all the advice Davy offered, or more clearly show the appropriateness of that advice for Coleridge. In the first stanza the speaker, like the one in Wordsworth's Ode, is the unbidden but undismissible guest at a vernal feast. The cause of his alienation in both poems is not, as in the conventional spring elegy, unrequited love but rather some failure of the general sensibility, the unwelcome discovery of the inability to feel that which intelligence and past experience assure the poet must be present. Thus far, and very little further, are the two poems congruent. The voice in Coleridge's poem that begins in conversational irony

('Well! if the Bard was weatherwise'), loses its composure and becomes a nearly hysterical shriek or groan—it is difficult to know which—within eighteen lines. And the occasion for this despair—'A Grief without a pang, void, dark, & drear'—is nowhere within the poem. It simply appears, abruptly, after the report on the weather, located neither in man nor atmosphere. The vain struggle to repress its stifling, drowsy, unimpassioned possession of the poet's sensibility—by the attempted surrender to the throstle in the larch tree, the wooing mild delights in all the tender sounds and gentle sights of the primrose month—appears in the lines of the poem. And although Coleridge speaks as if in opposition set against an enemy, the enemy is as much without as within, is as difficult to locate as the source of the lines that announce its presence.

To what extent do the verses create a mood at all? The frustration seems finally created by the desperate attempt to fill a page with lines of verse, to find something to say, or even something to talk about. The sky, of course, provides little distinction as a subject. Like the Mariner, at first watching the water snakes, this speaker can only statically exclaim (How ugly, or here, how beautiful) unless he can make distinctions, unless the moon moves or the eye loses its blankness. Outward forms, lifeless shapes, even the gentle thought of Sara, stir him feebly, feebly, feebly—the word is desperately repeated as though it were a slipping hand holding him back from wordlessness.

Then, as in 'Frost at Midnight', a moment of reminiscence earns a paragraph of sense. If Now is meaningless, the Past at least offers progression. But it is not, as in 'Frost at Midnight', a contrary that itself offers meaning. The contrast between Now and Then at first is an opportunity for the speaker to express a sort of contempt toward his own foolishness. Surely he asks that his pronouncement about 'the Man so stripp'd of good affections' be heard as an instance of adolescent fatuousness. Yet what began as an instance of fatuousness does indeed shortly become a Sweet Thought that lifts the weight, allows words to flow, makes possible now a paragraph of faery romance in which Sara is presented seated 'Upon the sod-built Seat of Camomile' where 'tho' thy Robin may have ceas'd to sing, / Yet needs for *my* sake must thou love to hear / The Bee-hive murmuring near.'

By imagining the absent loved one watching the same sky, moon, or star—using that persistent convention of easy love songs—the speaker constructs a conceit that is even less interesting here than when it was used for Charles Lamb five years before in 'This Lime-tree Bower My Prison' (in that poem the rook and setting sun at least are there to be pointed at):

> I feel my spirit moved—
> And wheresoe'er thou be,
> O Sister! O Beloved!
> Those dear wild Eyes, that see
> Even now the Heaven, *I* see—
> There is a Prayer in them! It is for *me*—
> And I, dear Sara—*I* am blessing *thee*!

The conceit in this poem is not really conclusive but permissive— it leads to and justifies the tableau of Mary, Sara and Coleridge before the low decaying fire, a scene perhaps enacted a few weeks earlier when Coleridge stopped at Gallow Hill on his way back to Keswick:

> O that affectionate & blameless Maid,
> Dear Mary! on her Lap my head she lay'd—
> Her Hand was on my Brow,
> Even as my own is now;
> And on my Cheek I felt thy eye-lash play.
> Such Joy I had, that I may truly say,
> My Spirit was awe-stricken with the Excess
> And trance-like Depth of it's brief Happiness.

The gesture in which the speaker lays his own hand on his brow is so appropriate to the tone of this letter and so obviously a part of the vision here that it seems almost certain that these lines were composed before the analogous ones in 'A Day Dream', where they are revised to stand explicitly as a fantasy. Probably as he revised the verse letter as 'Dejection' he attempted to retrieve these deleted lines and give them, in effect, a poem to themselves. But in the verse letter, of course, the day dream is not an isolated moment, a phenomenon to be described. Rather it is a means of introducing in his expression of his relationship to Sara, part of his apology for having written her a 'complaining Scroll / Which even to bodily Sickness bruis'd thy Soul!', and a way of stating his resolution not to let his heart 'in idle Wishes roam / Morbidly soft' when once Sara, Mary, Dorothy and William 'Shall dwell together in one happy Home, / One House the dear *abiding* Home of All.' And the more he talks to convince himself that his stance is rather heroic and to anticipate the possibility of a time when 'I too will crown me with a Coronal', the more the prospect of actually visiting amidst this bliss carries with it an anticipation of the pain of parting from it to return to 'My own peculiar Lot, my house-hold Life' characterized by 'Indifference or Strife'. And the attention to his own situation, here as in the other letters, provokes a flow of words beyond the control of literary order or taste:

> The transientness is Poison in the Wine,
> Eats out the pith of Joy, makes all Joy hollow,
> All Pleasure a dim Dream of Pain to follow! ...
> Wherefore, O wherefore! should I wish to be
> A wither'd branch upon a blossoming Tree?

This indulgence of self-pity is only a step, or a few lines, from the indulgence of self-inflicted pain—the vision of Sara ill and himself absent, 'To know that thou art weak & worn with pain, / And not to hear thee, Sara! not to view thee. ...'

Turning then again to listen to the now 'raving' wind is an attempt to dismiss the source of pain. He has now, it is true, written some 180 lines—some of it very bad verse by any standard, very little of it addressed to anything like the situation he vaguely set himself at the beginning of the poem. The attention paid to the wind *is* a change of direction in several senses. Now the attention is outward, the literary mode is deliberate and controlled—an address to a Muse, a search for an epithet, a seeking after narrative —who or what art thou, and 'what tell'st thou now about?' The poet is no longer in the passive state of a wind harp ('wherefore did I let it haunt my mind') but a man contemplating the sound made by a wind harp: 'What a Scream / Of agony by Torture

lengthen'd out / That Lute sent forth!' As so often in the almost
freely associated notebook passages, order is gained by making a
metaphor that merges the internal self with something perceived
in the external world. A notebook passage of 1803 (that
Humphry House discusses in a similar connection)[1] shows almost
the same process in prose: there as here the comments on the
raging wind accurately describe the linguistic behaviour of the
previous sentences: 'Storm all night—the wind scourging &
lashing the rain, with the pauses of self-wearying Violence that
returns to its wild work as if maddened by the necessity of the
Pause.' And there as here the poet, like the wind, is both driver
and driven; composition is a passive *and* active process to which
the self finds it almost impossible to be reconciled: 'I, half-dozing,
list'ning to the same, not without solicitations of the poetic
Feeling for / from I have written. . . .' The ambiguity of the last
two prepositions applies as usefully to the verse letter as to the
notebook entry—the act of composition for Coleridge is both
response and impulse. And the attempt to change the wind's
noise into a lyrical ballad—'as William's Self had made the tender
Lay'—seems to make possible, for a moment, one of the two
moments in the verse letter where Sara has an existence apart
from the poet's own; the delicate if weary prayer for her restful
sleep:

> O breathe She softly in her gentle Sleep!
> Cover her, gentle Sleep! with wings of Healing.
> And be this Tempest but a mountain Birth!
> May all the Stars hang bright about her Dwelling,
> Silent, as tho' they *watch'd* the sleeping Earth.
> Healthful & light, my Darling! may'st thou rise
>   With clear & chearful Eyes—
> And of the same good Tidings to me send!
>   For, oh! beloved Friend!
> I am not the buoyant Thing, I was of yore—
> When like an own Child, I to JOY belong'd;
> For others mourning oft, myself oft sorely wrong'd
> Yet bearing all things then, as if I nothing bore!

[1] House, *Coleridge*, pp. 23–6.

But again, by the dialectic that keeps this poem going, the act of rejoicing has called up the note of despair, and the syntax that embodies it, when the self-pity at the end of the passage above is under control, is that of Wordsworth's Ode:

> There *was* a time when tho' my path was rough,
> The Joy within me dallied with Distress,
> And all Misfortunes were but as the Stuff
> Whence Fancy made me Dreams of Happiness . . .
> But now Ill Tidings bow me down to earth/
> Nor care I, that they rob me of my Mirth/
> But oh! each Visitation
> Suspends what Nature gave me at my Birth,
> My shaping Spirit of Imagination!

Because here, at last, Coleridge directly attempts to understand what the first part of this poem was about, and to put together his sense of his poetic loss, his domestic strife, his devotion to the Wordsworth-Hutchinson circle, and the pattern of his own intellectual life for the past year (at least), it is inevitably important and inescapably confusing—not as finely rendered, or as obscure, as it appears in the final version of 'Dejection'.   *141494*

At first Coleridge insists that Ill Tidings, the suspending force (he tries several times to find the right name for the cause) do not mean the habitual Ills of a household of unequal minds, for that situation 'leaves me . . . Past care [or cure], & past Complaint' in a condition of austerity rather than fear. But the Wordsworth circle 'make up a world of Hopes & Fears for me', and thus produce an intensity of feeling beside which his 'coarse domestic life' can be seen as dulling and deadening, because it, in contrast to that of the Wordsworth household, offers 'No Habits of heart-nursing Sympathy / No Griefs' and 'No Hopes of its own Vintage . . . Whence when I mourn'd for you, My Heart might borrow / Fair forms & living Motions for it's Sorrow.'

The ill tidings, then, are apparently *not* directly the cause of the suspension of the shaping spirit of Imagination. Rather it is Coleridge's sense of his hopes and fears existing separately from the conditions of his daily life, his feeling of being divided between where he lives and where he feels, and—perhaps most

important—isolated as a *feeling* person from any mode of life
which can offer *forms* to combat, control and give shape and meaning to those feelings of Hope and Fear. It is as though a man faced
an armed enemy in a room in which all the weapons are locked in
cupboards. Or, if Hope not Fear is the occasion, he is most
simply an impotent lover. The condition of his life, he insists,
is a fragmentation of faculties, and its only remedy 'is not to
think of what I needs must feel', to obliterate, it would seem, his
sense of Sara Hutchinson and the Wordsworths but not Sara
Coleridge, by a devotion to 'abstruse Research'. And it is the
success of this 'sole Resource, my wisest plan' that Coleridge has
been mourning in this letter, which is not a love letter but an
explanation of his failure to write a love letter. Even his children,
simultaneously reminding him of the possibility of feeling and the
error of his marriage which has now become Necessity, are half-
regretted. It is the sad thoughts they bring that cause him, he says
in the least perceptive lines of the whole poem, to sing 'My love
song, with my breast against a Thorn'. Never was a poet less a
nightingale than Coleridge here.

In this and the following stanza, the relationship between
affliction, grief, love, joy, hope and fear—and the poet's sense of
his own anaesthetic state—becomes hopelessly obscure. Is he complaining of the feelings he has, or their absence? Lines can be
found which demonstrate either. Is it his feeling for the Wordsworth circle—or his failure to find such feeling—that oppresses
him? Again because the vocabulary is so uncertain the argument
can too easily go either way. So it is hardly surprising that in one
stanza the children should be a bliss that calls up a woe, in the next
a grief that awakens love and joy. Obviously a reader cannot come
to this poem for psychological or emotional—or finally linguistic
—consistency. The direct echo, with no real preparation at all, of
Wordsworth's Ode in this stanza is merely one more moment in
a poem without mode, in a form that allows any attitude if the
preceding words have somehow suggested it:

> These Mountains too, these Vales, these Woods, these Lakes,
> Scenes full of Beauty & of Loftiness

Where all my Life I fondly hop'd to live—
I were sunk low indeed, did they *no* solace give;
But oft I seem to feel, & evermore I fear,
They are not to me now the Things, which once they were.

This prosaic echoing of lines he probably first heard Wordsworth recite during the previous twenty-four hours (and that Wordsworth himself had known in Coleridge's 'Mad Monk') betrays the fact that this *is* to some extent a competitive poem, that one of its motives must have been Coleridge's urgent desire to prove that he too could find words for a spiritual crisis.

The famous section on giving and receiving life to and from nature, in this context, is all too familiar an idea. Except for the conceit of wedding garment and shroud, which a reader's memory of Blake's marriage hearse may cause to sound better than it should, the stanza is no more than a conventional description of the poet's genius, a restatement of the Preface to *Lyrical Ballads*, or the Ode. The Poet's soul issues forth a luminous cloud, a glory which enables him to behold 'aught . . . of higher Worth' and thus sets him apart from and above the 'loveless ever-anxious Crowd' who find only an inanimate cold world. 'Loveless' and 'ever-anxious', of course, are terms that simply, yet almost adequately, describe the state that Coleridge has been mourning in himself, and reflect the anxious suspicion that he may be no poet.

In the concluding address to Sara, Coleridge makes a final attempt to clarify the obscure vocabulary of this poem by stating now that her Joy is the light, the luminous cloud, the glory, the power of feeling (and presumably of writing) that he says has been denied or destroyed or perverted within himself. For the first time in the poem he acknowledges, though very indirectly, a responsibility for the failure, for Joy is a gift reserved for 'the Pure, & in their purest Hour'. The terms used for the state of his feelings and imagination are almost located in a specific relationship between people, but the poet's attempt to return to the earlier lines of the poem with this now more stable vocabulary is futile. The terms are definable here only because they are used in a different way.

But the eulogy of Sara with which the poem ends is separable from the formless mode of the rest of the poem, because it is a moment in which Sara is allowed to stand by herself as something other than an adjunct of the poet's self-pity: House rightly praises the image of the conjugal and mother dove, for it is an achievement of composition perhaps discovered at the expense of the poem's previous 500 lines. But it is an independence without resolution. The portrait of Sara, touched only slightly with envy, presents a woman who does partake of the world she expresses— the warmth of the dove's wings, the dove's affection. The Sara here is entirely reflexive, simultaneously giving and receiving, expressing and feeling. This power of innocence, to have the world become the eddying of one's living soul, is of course the solicitation of the poetic feeling for / from which Coleridge has been writing and which he here relinquishes for the sake of a poetics of composition rather than communion. That Coleridge later removed this passage, reclaimed the effort for himself, sent part of the poem to Poole and Southey as moments in a poem addressed respectively to Poole and to Wordsworth, does not diminish the moving achievement of its final lines in this form.

The most illuminating definition of the way the verse letter is constructed is Coleridge's own description of the absence of Method: 'an habitual submission of the understanding to mere events and images as such, and independent of any power in the mind to classify and appropriate them' (*Friend*, Section II, iv). The source, the starting point of Method, Coleridge says there, is the initiative to bring the disparate together—initiative based not simply on memory (which of itself is passive and leads to confusion) or passion, which can be a false initiative. Rather there must be a union of universal and particular that offers a continuous, progressive transition. Of course Coleridge, when he wrote the verses, had been discovering rather painfully that his method applied to himself was, for him now at least, an impossibility because there was no way in which he could make himself simultaneously the student and the object studied, and this poem by its failure justifies its argument. The verses to Sara, after all, are about what Coleridge was later to call the absence of initiative.

In the preceding year Coleridge had almost convinced himself, with the resources of philosophy as well as introspection, that the poet in him was dead and that he could find no literary way of achieving the necessary balance between the percipient and the perceived. Words, either because they are 'mere' words or because his demands on them are illegitimate, will not or cannot do what he asks of them. Despair, grief and love, for him, lack the deep and steady nature of 'genuinely' poetic feelings, and are merely transitory moments of sensation. On the other hand, clouds, green lights, children, storms, flickering eyelashes may be real things that because they are objective can become images or ideas, but they cannot be made into metaphors which allow the creation of an authentic 'I'. Nevertheless, 'almost with convulsive effort', Coleridge did manage to write an account of failure that, even if it is not a sublime ode, will within the next six months be rewritten as a poem of unique achievement. But perhaps the most important effect of the letter to Sara is that the dialogue with Wordsworth was kept open a bit longer, in a way that was to benefit enormously the course of English poetry.

Most of this dialogue must have been oral, and if no letters survive (or even were written) to indicate what was said in it, Dorothy's *Journal* at least indicates the occasions on which the poets met. Having composed the verse letter on April 4th, Coleridge apparently did not read it immediately to the Wordsworths. The next day Dorothy and William walked to Eusemere where she stayed with the Clarksons while William went (on April 7th, his thirty-second birthday) to spend five days with Mary at Middleham. After William rejoined Dorothy at Eusemere, on the 15th they walked home by way of Kirkstone Pass and apparently did not see Coleridge again until he unexpectedly visited them on April 20th, having stopped on his way to carve his name and Dorothy's over Sara's at Sara's Rock. On the morning of 21st April Coleridge came to William and Dorothy while they 'sauntered a little in the garden' of Town End and read to them—it was probably his first opportunity to do so since April 4th—'the verses he wrote to Sara'.

Given the fact that the first four stanzas of the 'Immortality'

Ode must have played some part in provoking this letter to Sara, to what extent can Coleridge be said to be answering Wordsworth while he was addressing Sara? Clearly here as elsewhere Coleridge shares Wordsworth's assumption that the loss of responsiveness is an event occurring within the poet over which he has very little control. And even though Wordsworth's completed Ode will make clear his belief that his own loss is due to a failed connection within an existing system, rather than (as it is for Coleridge) a catastrophe casting doubt on the validity of the system itself, Wordsworth does not suggest in those opening stanzas of the Ode, or in any poem of this period before 'Resolution and Independence', the possibility of belief in spite of evidence that denies it. The very desperation of 'The Rainbow' implies that Wordsworth's doubt was then as radical as Coleridge's, and the single tree, in the Ode, raises briefly but forcefully an anxiety that, in Coleridge's letter, becomes almost a terror—the fearful possibility that objects, even natural ones, may have their fullest existence outside, beyond the reach of any system within which a man may include himself. In being 'not Man's hills, but all for themselves' (as Dorothy was to write two weeks later), such objects for a humanist are merely chaos, and to a man is left, as a form of controlling order, only society, his relationships with other men. The 'festival' of the second and third stanzas of Wordsworth's Ode, by virtue of which the poet temporarily earns his coronal, at first assumes an orderly reality that appears comprehensive, full of the life, sound, motion, winds that make May in every sense a holiday. But the one object separated, the Tree that becomes of many one, a field that is single, can cast the observer back upon himself, destroy his role as celebrant, thrust him forth into a world of contending realities in which such order is merely a poet's dream.

It is as an outcast, in these terms of Wordsworth's, that Coleridge begins addressing Sara, and the suspended storm is the converse of Wordsworth's May Day exultation. The mood with which the letter opens, then, is the symptom of the speaker's having been cast back upon himself as sole resource, and the letter is an extended plea for some new form of unequivocal connection, a vain hope to be shocked back into a single reality by storm or, failing that, to be welcomed into a society of human love as a member of that tableau before the hearth. The green light, the playing eyelash, the guileless letter, his children, are all things that promise to be more than objects, promise connection. But they fail to yield it. Like the mountains, vales, woods, lakes they 'are not to me now the Things, which once they were' just as to Wordsworth the meadow, grove, stream and 'every common sight' are 'The things which I have seen [and] I now can see no more'. Things, seen or not seen, represent failure in these two poems as they did in Coleridge's letters of the preceding year. And Coleridge's final blessing of Sara is a recognition, even an envious recognition, of her participation in a world where things have meaning as parts of a relation that is sacramental as well as social:

> JOY! Sara! is the Spirit & the Power,
> That wedding Nature to us gives in Dower
> A new Earth and new Heaven.

Sara's social relations—the wedding, the 'conjugal & mother Dove'—are transcended by the 'Suffusion of that Light', but his— 'Sister & Friend of my devoutest Choice'—leave him perilously close to 'the poor loveless ever-anxious Crowd' who dwell singly and frigidly in 'that inanimate cold World' of contending realities. For both Wordsworth and Coleridge the communion from which they have been exiled is social as well as spiritual, though the community in Wordsworth's Ode is abstract and general (May celebrants) rather than specific and particular—the households at Grasmere and Keswick. For Wordsworth the possibility of actual domestic exile never enters the Ode or any of the poems of this period. Indeed the prospect of his marriage to Mary is seen as an extension to her of a social concord that exists fully for him already. The festival is a social metaphor for a state of mind, not as for Coleridge a social analogue and perhaps cause. For all Coleridge's insistence on the subjective origin of joy, much of the verse letter works in quite a different direction—toward a conclusion that is unresolvable because it depends on outside intervention. But not until 'Resolution and Independence' does Wordsworth confront this question in terms that comprehend

Coleridge's sense of exclusion as well as that more general sense he presents in the first four stanzas of his own Ode. And the lyric form of the Ode, which Coleridge implicitly questions in the verse letter by dealing with experience sequentially as the contradictory chaotic flow of an individual consciousness, Wordsworth discards in favour of the resolution that a new sort of autobiographical narrative offers, a mode that only appears at transitory moments in Coleridge's 'Verses to Sara'.

Although the record of Wordsworth's literary and social activities in the weeks that intervene between Coleridge's verse letter and his own 'Resolution and Independence' becomes increasingly full, Coleridge almost disappears. None of his surviving letters were written during or allude to this period, and the notebook entries for the month are brief and enigmatic. The lack of information about Coleridge may be accidental: part of the time William and Dorothy are travelling and simply out of touch with him. When they returned to Grasmere on April 16th, Dorothy writes to Mary, they found a letter from Coleridge telling them that 'he has been ailing for two or 3 days'. 'This is sad news,' Dorothy remarks, 'poor fellow! I fear he has his own torments.' William's answer to Coleridge's letter survives, the only one to Coleridge in 1802 that does, but Wordsworth's concern with his own activities leaves little opportunity for much of a response to Coleridge's matter or his tone. Apparently this letter from Coleridge (or the one Dorothy received on April 13th), like William's reply, contained verses. But William's comment on these are perfunctory: one fragment has 'admirable simplicity in the language'; he wishes he had more of the second, though the fourth line wants mending sadly'; the extract from Pliny is 'very judicious'. (In a notebook two years earlier Coleridge had copied out Pliny's advice that a writer who wishes to be universally and forever admired should 'revise repeatedly, and in consultation with numerous advisers'—NB, 693.) What Coleridge's fragments may have been is mysterious: he later sent parts of the 'Verses to Sara' to other correspondents as 'fragments', but surely these would have occasioned more comment from Wordsworth, or at least from Dorothy. The notebooks for the period after his return to Keswick in mid-March sketch several prospective poems, which, if ever written, do not survive.

The probability that William and Dorothy first heard the 'Verses to Sara,' on the morning of April 21st is increased by the tonal intensity of Dorothy's written response to them, recorded in the *Journal*:

I was affected with them, and was on the whole, not being well, in miserable spirits. The sunshine, the green fields, and the fair sky made me sadder; even the little happy, sporting lambs seemed but sorrowful to me. The pile wort spread out on the grass a thousand shining stars. . . . I went to bed after dinner, could not sleep, went to bed again. Read Ferguson's life and a poem or two—fell asleep for 5 minutes and awoke better. . . .

The number of connections that can be drawn between Dorothy's brief account of her response to Coleridge's poem and William's own poems of the same period is astonishing. Although the thought of grief in the midst of green fields and sporting lambs is certainly a recollection of the situation in the opening of the 'Immortality' Ode, which William had begun a month earlier, it also anticipates the fourth and fifth stanzas of 'Resolution and Independence', which William would begin in a fortnight. Robert Ferguson, who was said to have been Scotland's leading poet at the age of twenty-one and who died mad three years later (in 1774), is as relevant as Chatterton and Burns to stanza VII of the same poem. And the pile wort, spread like a thousand shining stars, is the Small Celandine, about which William would write two poems in a week's time, one of them using this star analogy.

The six weeks of this spring, the period between Wordsworth's first attempt at the 'Immortality' Ode and his beginning of 'Resolution and Independence', tempt the biographer because they so obviously represent a personal crisis involving the lives of at least three people. But the weeks are irresistibly fascinating to the literary critic because these personal crises are so obviously reflected in, if indeed not conducted in, the words that survive in the letters, notebooks, journals and magnificent poems of the people involved.

CHAPTER IV

The Elegiac Spring

COLERIDGE'S propensity for uninhibited self-interest and uncritical self-expression must often have been an embarrassment to the Wordsworth household. Whatever terms they chose for expressing the conduct of their own lives, they must have thought that a position like that which Coleridge takes, language such as he uses, in the verse letter to Sara was not appropriate to poetry or useful in the decorous conduct of everyday life. When Dorothy Wordsworth told Mary Hutchinson (on April 16th) to 'seek quiet or rather amusing thoughts' as an antidote to anxious love, she probably had not yet heard Coleridge's 'Verses to Sara' (though Mary may have read them), and her tone may well have been patronizing, adapted to what she assumed to be the weaker sensibility of her brother's bride. But the counsel of obliquity which follows in her letter to Mary has reference to the lives of William, Dorothy and Coleridge in a way that Mary was probably not expected to understand. 'Study the flowers,' Dorothy tells Mary, 'the birds and all the common things that are about you. O Mary, my dear Sister! be quiet and happy. Take care of yourself—keep yourself employed without fatigue, and do not make loving us your business, but let your love of us make up the spirit of all the business you have.' To Mary perhaps this advice is platitudinous, but it describes exactly the sort of concern that dominates the poetry William wrote during the six weeks that intervened between the composition of the first four stanzas of the 'Immortality' Ode (from March 27th) and the beginning of 'Resolution and Independence' (on May 3rd). The advice seems particularly pointed as an alternative to the indulgent pouring forth of Coleridge, and decorously appropriate as a way of proceeding for a brother and sister who could hardly make loving one another their business. If Coleridge's verse letter to Sara is an introspective excuse for his failure to write a love letter (or a love poem), many of the dozen or so poems Wordsworth wrote during this six-week period are oblique encounters both with the expression of love and the process of introspection. In them the ostensible business is indeed the study of birds, flowers, and 'common things', but their interest as poems comes from the fact that this 'study' is informed, its spirit is made up of matters less easily and directly expressed: William's love for Dorothy, his affection for Mary, his passionate anxiety about his own state as man and poet.

For some of these poems, such as 'The Glow-worm', the circumstances of composition are easily reconstructed; for others, such as 'The Linnet', only a rough guess about place and date can be made. Although 'The Tinker' is one rather tired attempt to revive the *Lyrical Ballad* style, the rest of the poems are deliberate though oblique confrontations of the questions raised and unanswered by the fragmentary opening of the Ode that William had composed a few weeks earlier. In them Wordsworth seems to be asking what literary modes offer a chance for the completeness and fullness of expression that the Ode so far lacks: how extensive a moment, how intense an experience, can be given a form that does not destroy that experience with a finality that is purely rhetorical, or dissipate its intensity into a formlessness like that of Coleridge's 'Verses to Sara'. The abstract generality of 'The Rainbow', for instance, was composed in a mode both autobiographical and lyrical, but the poem obviously suffered from a vagueness that Wordsworth must have found unsatisfying. Yet a poem such as 'The Cock is Crowing', written on April 16th while William and Dorothy were returning to Grasmere from Eusemere after William's visit to Mary, commemorates 'spontaneously' a moment of that extraordinarily fine spring in language far less engaging and interesting than that Dorothy uses in her *Journal* for the same occasion. In 'The Robin and the Butterfly' the experiment in modes is conducted not as a matter of rhyme and metre but as the making of epithets. In fact Dorothy later speaks of William's having 'teased himself with seeking for an epithet for the cuckoo' as though such experiments were a kind of out-of-door parlour game they often played. The epithet, like the epitaph, is a gesture by which, through the tender fiction of the imagination, one personates not the deceased but a fictitious relationship to a remote form of existence.

But several of the other poems of the same period are so intensely autobiographical that the moment commemorated is obscure, unarticulated. 'I have thoughts that are fed by the sun', for instance, celebrates silence in a way that makes life and death almost equivalent forms of peace, at the same time that the lines deny that such an equation can be made:

> My chamber is hush'd and still,
>   And I am alone,
>   Happy and alone.
>
> Oh! who would be afraid of life?
> The passion, the sorrow and the strife,
>   When he may lie
>   Shelter'd so easily?
> May lie in peace on his bed.
> Happy as they who are dead.
> O life, there is about thee
> A deep delicious peace,
> I would not be without thee,
>   Stay, Oh Stay!
> Yet be thou ever as now,
> Sweetness and breath with the quiet of death,
>   Peace, peace, peace.

The connection between this poem and Dorothy is more apparent when it is compared with the lines Dorothy used to soothe her distraught brother on May 4th, after he had begun 'Resolution and Independence': here too a kind of articulate silence takes possession of the speaker's sensibility, and he replaces the perceived world with an enjoyment of absolute security that he shares with his sister:

> This is the spot;—how mildly does the sun
> Shine in between the fading leaves! The air
> In the habitual silence of this wood
> Is more than silent; and this bed of heath—

Where shall we find so sweet a resting place?
Come!—let me see thee sink into a dream
Of quiet thoughts—protracted till thine eye
Be calm as water, when the winds are gone
And no one can tell whither—My sweet Friend,
We too have had such happy hours together
That my heart melts in me to think of it.

The sort of moment that both fragments commemorate is presumably the kind that Dorothy describes on April 29th, when she and William went to John's Grove:

... William lay, and I lay, in the trench under the fence—he with his eyes shut, and listening to the waterfalls and the birds. There was no one waterfall above another—it was a sound of waters in the air—the voice of the air. William heard me breathing and rustling now and then, but we both lay still, and unseen by one another; he thought that it would be as sweet thus to lie so in the grave, to hear the *peaceful* sounds of the earth, and just to know that our dear friends were near.

But as Coleridge had shown in the 'Verses to Sara', as Wordsworth demonstrates in these two fragments, it is impossible virtually to deny consciousness and still write poetry. For both poets the failure to be articulate results from a failure to find the analogous mode for a fantasy (or a passion) that has itself no words to utter. In neither case is there anything for the poet to attend to, listen for, look at, expect or remember. 'Things', to Coleridge too often (for the sake of his poetry) became the forms of abstraction or the formlessness of grief.

But Wordsworth, when he made an effort—or perhaps when his sister made an effort for him—could and did attend. If Wordsworth's poems during this six-week period were conceived in anxious apprehension about Annette, Mary, Dorothy—his past, his future, his art—and if he seems always about to suggest in them that the answer to the trials of existence is oblivion, the most interesting of the poems find their life and being in something far different. 'The Glow-worm' is perhaps as useful an example as any of them, because so much is known about its composition and its immediate effect. Wordsworth began the

poem, he told his sister, while watering his horse in Lord Darlington's park just after leaving Mary at Middleham on April 12th,
and the circumstance of its composition Dorothy felt was significant enough to describe at some length, on April 20th:

Just when William came to a well or a trough, which there is in Lord
Darlington's park, he began to write that poem of *The Glow-worm*,
not being able to ride upon the long trot—interrupted in going
through the town of Staindrop, finished it about 2 miles and a half
beyond Staindrop. He did not feel the jogging of the horse while he was
writing; but, when he had done, he felt the effect of it, and his fingers
were cold with his gloves. His horse fell with him on the other side of
St. Helen's, Auckland. So much for *The Glow-worm*.

William too recounted the circumstance to Coleridge when he
sent him a copy of it on April 16th, remarking that 'The incident
of this Poem took place about seven years ago between Dorothy
and me'. Though William too seems most concerned with the
oddness of the physical circumstances, its being written during
a horseback journey, Dorothy was obviously moved by the
poem itself, and undoubtedly heard it as a tribute to her: she
repeats it to herself as she walks along by the foot of Brother's
Water (on April 16th), copied it out for Mary in her letter of the
same evening (with no comment, perhaps as an afterthought),
repeated it again with William on April 20th.

   Why should the poem have occasioned so much concern? It is,
after all, a simple enough statement: a man riding on a stormy
night finds a glow-worm and takes it home for his Love because
she has never seen one; the next evening they both enjoy finding
it where he had left it the night before. Yet its tone makes it
clearly an oblique love poem: the speaker's recognizing the glow-
worm as a possible gift implies a concern for the beloved, and the
survival of the insect is proof that natural blessing has been be-
stowed on their love, as he suggests by his solicitude:

> I laid the Glowworm gently on a leaf,
> And bore it with me through the stormy night
> In my left hand—without dismay or grief
> Shining, albeit with a fainter light.   (letter version)

And the excessive anxiety about its survival is finally compensated by Emma's joy in seeing it:

> The whole next day I hop'd, and hop'd with fear:
> At night the Glowworm shone beneath the Tree;
> I led my Emma to the place,—"Look here!"—
> O joy it was for her, and joy for me! (letter version)

Certainly William had written oblique love poems to Dorothy before this, but this poem was written only a few hours after he had left Mary, as he was returning from an apparently urgent visit occasioned by William and Dorothy's conclusion a few weeks earlier that the wedding would take place after William and Dorothy went to France to see Annette and Caroline. If Dorothy had begun to experience early the anxieties about William's marriage that are expressed so vividly in her subsequent account of the days in October, this poem alluding to their first years of living together at Racedown must have been offered by William as a kind of reassurance—which makes Dorothy's sending it immediately to Mary something less than generous-spirited. In the text of the poem that Sara Hutchinson preserved that spring in the notebook called *Sara's Poets*, 'Mary' is substituted for 'Emma'—which suggests that Sara may have been aware of some ambiguity, perhaps even tried to correct it.

And more important, for literary history at least, 'The Glow-worm' marks that fuller subordination of William's sensibility to Dorothy's that sets the tone for much of the next few weeks' composition. On the fifteenth of April, when they set out from Eusemere by way of Gowbarrow Park, Dorothy notices 'that starry yellow flower which Mrs. C. calls pile wort', and which William within a fortnight will address as 'The Small Celandine'. A few miles further along Ullswater she sees by the water-side a crowd of daffodils:

They grew among the mossy stones about and about them; some rested their heads upon these stones as on a pillow for weariness; and the rest tossed and reeled and danced, and seemed as if they verily laughed with the wind, that blew upon them over the lake; they looked so gay, ever glancing, ever changing. This wind blew directly over the

lake to them. There was here and there a little knot, and a few stragglers
a few yards higher up; but they were so few as not to disturb the
simplicity, unity, and life of that one busy highway.

Although William will not write 'I Wandered Lonely as a
Cloud' for two more years, his account will closely echo the
language as well as the situation of Dorothy's description. That
journey home to Grasmere, and the close association between
brother and sister in the succeeding weeks, obviously helped to
stimulate literary activity for both of them. Dorothy's observa-
tions in her *Journal* are keener and more prolific than at any other
time, and her conversations with William clearly helped to set
him writing. Moreover Dorothy is both conscious and proud of
her power. Her last sentence on April 17th is simply, 'I saw a robin
chacing a scarlet butterfly this morning.' The next morning, 'We
sate in the Orchard. William wrote the poem on *The Robin and
the Butterfly*.' Or ten days later, 'I happened to say that when I was
a child I would not have pulled a strawberry blossom. ... At
dinner time he came in with the poem of *Children gathering
Flowers*.'

The counsel of obliquity which Dorothy had given Mary in
her letter of April 16th is now fully manifest in William's poems.
The attitudes expressed in March—vaguely as 'natural piety',
whimsically as hospitality and nostalgia (the first poem 'To a
Butterfly' and 'To the Cuckoo')—are now more explicitly protective. The poet hesitates to confront the natural violence and hostility in 'The Robin and the Butterfly' ('A brother he seems of thine
own / ... Love him, or leave him alone'), but the whole effort of
the poems to a Daisy (or the Lark, the Linnet, the Celandine) is to
find an epithet that humanizes, controls and protects the object
observed, and consequently the emotion of the observer. The
first poem to the daisy, for instance, begins with the situation of
the 'Immortality' Ode (a connection that Wordsworth himself
made in the epigraph of 1815):

> In youth from rock to rock I went,
> From hill to hill in discontent
> Of pleasure high and turbulent,
>   Most pleased when most uneasy. ...

But now the daisy offers a delight that is tranquil and restorative, a 'happy, genial influence' that is mysterious but welcome, and vaguely anticipates the resolution later achieved when the Ode was completed:

> A thousand times in rock or bower,
> Ere thus I have lain couched an hour
> Have I derived from thy sweet power
>   Some apprehension;
> Some steady love; some chance delight;
> Some memory that had taken flight
> Some chime of fancy wrong or right;
>   Or stray invention.
>
> If stately passions in me burn,
> And some chance look to Thee should turn,
> I drink out of an humbler urn
>   A lowlier pleasure;
> The homely sympathy that heeds
> The common life our nature breeds;
> A wisdom fitted to the needs
>   Of hearts at leisure.   (MS. version.)

The calming influence—even the language echoes Dorothy's advice to Mary—is an antidote to passion and an alternative (as a phrase later altered makes explicit) to true devotion. When the daisy becomes in the second poem even more anthropomorphic, it is difficult not to see its mild-mannered, retiring ordinariness as a kind of metaphor for Mary, as though Wordsworth too were deliberately setting out to write, as Coleridge once planned to, about one in whom he 'can see nothing extraordinary . . .—a Poem noting all the virtues of the mild & retired kind'. The great virtue of the daisy's mildness, as Wordsworth suggests in the poem 'To the Same Flower', is that it can be called almost anything, 'as is the humour of the game': a nun demure, a sprightly maiden, a queen in crown of rubies dresst, a starvelling, a cyclops, a shield, 'a pretty star / Not quite so fair as many are / In heaven above thee.' Given 'a sweet silent creature' as subject, the poet has only to indulge his own whimsy in order to make a poem, to 'repair [his] heart with gladness'.

9

Dorothy, on the one hand, counselled obliquity—letting love become the spirit of the everyday, rather than letting passion replace and subordinate the everyday and become a business in itself. Coleridge, however, wrote his 'Verses to Sara' as though existence was only passion, or the pain caused by its absence. In their midst Wordsworth, perhaps with some discomfort, spent many hours writing poems that must have seemed inadequate replies to both forms of counsel. It is obviously more than a coincidence that the concerns of William, Dorothy, and Coleridge should exhibit such curious parallels during these weeks. Dorothy's *Journal* shows that they shared their distresses and their remedies— that when she lay on her bed reading the life of Ferguson and trying to sleep away her misery after hearing Coleridge repeat his 'Verses to Sara', the other two knew what she was suffering and doing. The notion of using poetic control as a means of alleviating distress must have been as frequent a subject of conversation as of literary experimentation. The differences between Wordsworth's loss of responsiveness described in the Ode, and Coleridge's as expressed in the various versions of 'Dejection', have been end-lessly defined. But the differences in their approach to 'Nature' seem far less significant than the fact that they shared with one another, and with Dorothy, an apprehension about their im-mediate futures. Coleridge's sense of domestic chaos, balanced against his impossible affection for Sara Hutchinson and his envy of the Wordsworth household, was explicit and immediate, described in letters and verse. The 'Verses to Sara', the parallel concerns in 'The Picture' and 'A Day Dream', show to a modern reader—and must have shown even more clearly to the Words-worths—his continuing preoccupation with poetry as a means of control.

The sources of distress, and the means to alleviate it, at Grasmere are less publicly expressed, but undeniably present. The distance from the obliquity of 'To a Daisy' to that of Coleridge's 'The Picture' is enormous, but there are enough echoes to suggest that they share a dedication to 'emancipating the soul', whether from daydreams or from stately passions. Coleridge's disconsolate lover is the creature of maudlin romance, his landscape oddly constructed of careful observation and easy mythologizing, his creator's diction elaborate, elegant and whimsical. But with all this wordy circumstance his narrator, like Wordsworth's, seeks a situation in which he '... can now / With my own Fancies play the merry Fool, / And laugh away worse folly, being free.' Both of Wordsworth's poems to a Daisy separate attitudes, focus attention differently and precisely—but Coleridge's poem of almost two hundred lines includes everything from promiscuous fancy to careful observation of common things. Yet the search, along different paths, for resolution and independence informs both. Which of the poems came first is irrelevant—what matters here is that they must have grown out of conversations of intense personal interest to both poets. And if Wordsworth's role in these conversations must be left to conjecture, Dorothy's *Journal* more than once suggests that her brother's literary statements, and presumably his conversational ones as well, are often formal, more public articulations of the hopes and anxieties she expresses to herself more privately. No one can prove that the direction of Wordsworth's poetry during these important weeks was the result of Dorothy's insistence, just as no one can prove that the interplay between William and Coleridge was conducted primarily through Dorothy. But both conclusions seem almost inevitable for anyone who reads the poems, letters, journals and notebooks. It seems inadequate to speak of her as a 'creative catalyst'—her role seems to have been far more active and important than that. The formal tone of William's one surviving letter to Coleridge from the period (that of April 16th), the fact that it is to Dorothy that Coleridge sent his poems, the fact that she is the one who resolved to go to Keswick on May 15th when she was distressed by a melancholy letter, the similarity of their accounts of April 23rd, the recollection that William mocked his sister's tears ('nervous blubbering') the previous November when Coleridge left for London—all these suggest that significant communication not in verse between Grasmere and Keswick depended almost entirely on her.

Consider, for instance, the important part she plays in the lives of both poets during the last week in April, the week before

Wordsworth began writing 'Resolution and Independence'. On the 23rd, 'it being a beautiful morning', William, Dorothy and Coleridge start out walking toward Rydal but turn north toward Nab Scar. Leaving William 'feasting with silence', Dorothy and Coleridge push on to a rocky seat that reminds them of Andrew's broom (in the 'Oak and the Broom') and William's eglantine (in both 'The Waterfall and the Eglantine' and ''Tis said that some have died for love'). Here they sit, until they are rejoined by William who 'repeat[s] his poems'—probably these—and then the three linger to look below them at the vales: Rydal and Rydal Water to the south and east, beyond it Ambleside and the northern end of Windermere, then to the west Grasmere and its lake, and far to the southwest Coniston Fells. The scene Dorothy describes is in turn pastoral, domestic and wild: the houses and green fields of Ambleside; Grasmere from this perspective without houses or fields but a lake 'of nature's own' enclosed with bare hills, and the Fells 'in their own shape and colour—not Man's hills, but all for themselves, the sky and clouds, and a few wild creatures'. Meanwhile Coleridge had gone off by himself and soon calls them to come and see what he called the Double Bower—a 'sweet' enclosure of rock and ivy looking down on Ambleside, and above it a second resting place, a 'little parlour' covered by 'a sweet moss carpet'. They wish, of course, that Mary and Sara shared their discovery, and thus resolve to commemorate this moment next day with flowers. Coleridge's interest in the spot, his description of it in his notebook, and the probability that he listened that afternoon to William reciting ''Tis said that some have died for love' all make it likely that he used this experience in writing 'The Picture'. Dorothy's prose continually suggests ways in which a day spent like this was for the three of them a social occasion, an aesthetic experience, and a moment in which the three observers are separated from one another and their surroundings, yet in separation are brought closer to one another and to the world. This day, convenient to choose because both Dorothy and Coleridge left a record of it, undoubtedly shared its pattern with many others, as such their walks into Easedale and to Rydal on the days preceding and following.

After Coleridge left them on Sunday, the 25th, the activities of William and Dorothy are at first more narrowly domestic and literary. They read Spenser's *Prothalamion* in their orchard (Sunday), William works on 'The Tinker' and 'Children Gathering Flowers' (Tuesday and Wednesday), and on Thursday they read the verses Coleridge sent them. Until Thursday, Dorothy does little more than list their activities and note the weather. But on that day, after William has finally finished 'The Tinker', the account of their activities is more interesting. Brother and sister lie side by side next to the fence in John's Grove and imagine they are dead, listening to 'the *peaceful* sounds of the earth'. Lying 'still and unseen by one another', William listens while Dorothy observes: the colour of Silver How, the lambs on the island in the middle of Grasmere Lake, and later in the day 'the glittering silver line on the ridge of the backs of the sheep'. Then they return early, because Dorothy is 'sick and ill' after an afternoon visit to the Simpsons, to find a letter Fletcher has brought from Coleridge which disturbs William and leaves him, next day, with a headache.

But on Friday, in spite of the headache, William spends most of the day working on 'The Celandine', walking backwards and forwards in the orchard with Dorothy and repeating parts of it to her, much as they had read the *Prothalamion* together in the same spot earlier in the week. After a late dinner they go up into the Hollins, and spread the fur gown on the ground where William, still distressed by his headache, sleeps. But Dorothy 'lay with half-shut eyes looking at the prospect as in a vision almost', and composes a scene with Loughrigg Fell and Grasmere as its background, its foreground a 'wild intermixture of rocks, tree, and slacks of grassy ground'. This vision, and the scene of the church in the vale, make it 'a blessed place' in which even the thrush's song seems unnaturally loud.

The following day, equally fine, William and Dorothy again spend in one another's company—'sowing the scarlet beans' and flowers, sitting in the heat of the sun in the orchard while William continues to work on 'The Celandine', returning in the afternoon to their spot in the Hollins where again the scene is transformed for Dorothy: '. . . we saw nothing but the holly tree. . . . But that holly tree had a beauty about it more than its own, knowing as we did where we were.' From the rock shade, Dorothy is struck by 'the overwhelming beauty of the vale below', by the light reflected by the wings and bellies of two ravens, and by the last glimpse of the setting sun over Loughrigg Fell. And because they had left behind 'the poem' (presumably 'The Celandine') they return after tea to see 'sheep and lambs quiet among the rocks' in a fading landscape, a cloudless sky with three stars in the centre of its blue vault. And William, when they returned to the house, wrote the second part of 'The Celandine', in celebration of 'Pleasures newly found' through the medium of a flower for which notoriety is unnecessary: 'Praise it is enough for me, / If there be but three or four / Who will love my little Flower.'

The fact that an account from Dorothy's point of view is the only record for these days inevitably makes her presence felt in everything that was done or written. But her importance here is more than simply that of narrator, as it is elsewhere in the *Journal*. She continually shapes subjects, composes scenes, actively responds with words while William listens to the silence. When William writes, she is never far away—she listens to him compose, reads to him, suggests occasions for poems, reminds him of the experience he has shared with her, delights in and repeats what he finishes. If elsewhere in the *Journal* she seems primarily protective of her brother, here she encourages and influences. And the poems bear the mark of this influence, this encouragement to use 'the common things' as subject and control. William, by himself, one can imagine indulging in silence and oblivion were it not for Dorothy. To let love 'make up the spirit of all the business you have' rather than be a business itself must have been her advice to more than Mary.

Wordsworth's subordination—if that is the word for it—to his sister's sensibility was short-lived. The act of freeing himself from this dependence, whether deliberately or unconsciously, was the composition of his finest short poem, which seems to bring together all that Wordsworth had known and wanted to be since they came to Grasmere. It is one of the few poems in English that convincingly dramatizes, with astonishing economy, the transition from despair and dejection to confidence and triumph. Dorothy oddly absents herself from the circumstance of the composition of 'Resolution and Independence', as though she recognized that this was an autonomous poem rather than a co-operative enterprise. And it is the poem of Wordsworth's in which he is most obviously, insistently alone, as he reflects on but surpasses in every way the work he had been doing during the previous weeks. In subject, mood, comprehensiveness of vision, it seems far beyond the range of Dorothy's fine imagination. Her account for Sunday, May 2nd, is unusually brief: 'Again a heavenly morning. Letter from Coleridge.' And for Monday there is no account at all in her *Journal*. But from Tuesday's entry it is clear that on that Monday, after a week of fine weather spent almost constantly out of doors with Dorothy while he worked steadily and peacefully, William began the most significant of his shorter poems, which in the coming six weeks he will work at, revise, explain and defend: the poem he referred to as 'The Leechgatherer' but finally entitled 'Resolution and Independence'.

At no other period in his career did Wordsworth try more energetically to justify himself—to his sister, to Mary and Sara Hutchinson, to Annette, to Coleridge, to John Wilson, to his barber—as a poet, as a man, as a brother, perhaps as a husband. In the letter he and Dorothy composed for John Wilson in early June, for instance, his defence of 'The Idiot Boy' against Wilson's distaste is made the occasion for justifying a whole poetic career, a theory of literature, a moral scheme, even his own deficiencies as a letter writer. However fine the sentences in this letter are, its whole tone is in every sense defensive, yet relentlessly unapologetic. In a letter to Mary he similarly, but more briefly, defends 'Farewell to Grasmere', implying that Dorothy and Coleridge too had failed to understand it. But the most insistent defence of all is that written to Sara Hutchinson on June 14th, provoked by her objections to 'The Leechgatherer'. Here he bluntly tells her what the poem is supposed to mean and do:

... I describe myself as having been exalted to the highest pitch of delight by the joyousness and beauty of Nature; and then as depressed, even in the midst of those beautiful objects, to the lowest dejection and despair. A young Poet in the midst of the happiness of Nature is described as overwhelmed by the thoughts of the miserable reverses which have befallen the happiest of all men, *viz.* Poets. . . . A person reading the Poem with feelings like mine will have been awed and controuled, expecting almost something spiritual or supernatural. . . . You speak of [the old man's] speech as tedious: everything is tedious when one does not read with the feelings of the Author. '*The Thorn*' is tedious to hundreds; and so is the *Idiot Boy* to hundreds. It is in the character of the old man to tell his story in a manner which an *impatient* reader must necessarily feel as tedious. But Good God! Such a figure, in such a place, a pious self-respecting, miserably infirm and pleased old man telling such a tale! . . .

And Dorothy adds to William's chastisement a schoolmistressy note of her own:

When you happen to be displeased with what you suppose to be the tendency or moral of any poem which William writes, ask yourself whether you have hit upon the real tendency and true moral, and above all never think that he writes for no reason but merely because a thing happened . . .

For Sara to accept easily her sister's marrying into a household with defences of solidarity this sturdy suggests either enormous tolerance or an obliviousness no one else has ascribed to her. Impassioned pleas for love from Keswick, balanced by impassioned scoldings from Grasmere, must have made even Gallow Hill something of a sanctuary not lightly relinquished.

Wordsworth's motive in defending 'The Leechgatherer' to the Hutchinson sisters is implicit in the intensity of the poem itself. Clearly it is Wordsworth's most ambitious, and most successful, attempt to put together in a comprehensive form the world he occupied in life, in England, in the history of literature, at a moment when that world was about to change drastically.

The narrative organization of the poem, adapted from Dorothy's account of meeting a leechgatherer in the *Journal* of October 1800, does not sufficiently explain how it moves from line to line; and the Hutchinsons' questions apparently reflect their disappointed expectations for a story about a man, even another

Cumberland Beggar. Wordsworth's exasperation, then, expresses his inability to make them see that it is a poem about *his* feelings, not the leechgatherer's character. In his note on the poem dictated to Isabella Fenwick in 1842–3, Wordsworth carefully distinguished between the incident described by Dorothy and a subsequent, presumably more important occasion.

I was in the state of feeling described in the beginning of the poem, while crossing over Barton Fell from Mr. Clarkson's, at the foot of Ullswater towards Askam. The image of the hare I then observed on the ridge of the Fell.

Though Wordsworth remembers the poem as having been written in 1807, the circumstances involved with his 'state of feeling' seem to have survived more vividly in his mind than the date. The most obvious time for him to have been crossing Barton Fell must have been the visit he and Dorothy paid to the Clarksons at Eusemere in April 1802. (On their earlier visit, William and Dorothy on New Year's Day walked across Barton Fell towards Martindale, but the opening of the poem hardly suggests a wintry landscape.) And the most likely occasion during that visit was the day William left for Middleham to see Mary—April 7th, his thirty-second birthday. Though Dorothy says she walked six miles with him, she never indicates what direction they took—whether to Penrith, to take the stage, or directly across the fells to Askham, the River Lowther, and the main road. Though he had probably not yet heard Coleridge's 'Verses to Sara', Wordsworth, on his thirty-second birthday, going to meet the woman he had promised to marry, about to cross through or near the estate of Lord Lonsdale, the man who had been responsible for his own financial distress, might well have thought of the anxious prospects facing a poet. The poem's antecedents in Wordsworth's reading and writing, its genesis in his literary and personal encounters with Coleridge, help to explain his attitude in the letter and elsewhere that says, rather arrogantly, 'if you know not this, you know not me'.

More explicitly than the 'Verses to Sara', more obviously than the first stanzas of the 'Immortality' Ode, the poem begins by

invoking the situation of the spring elegy, a form Wordsworth
had encountered repeatedly in the work of Bruce, Graeme,
Langhorne, John Scott and Ferguson (most of these in Anderson's
British Poets): a young man, at first exulting in spring, feels suddenly
and painfully a sense of his distance from the mood of the season.
Usually the speaker is a rejected lover, like the one in Bruce's
'Elegy—Written in Spring,' who finds that

> Now Spring returns; but not to me returns
>   The vernal joy my better years have known;
> Dim in my breast life's dying taper burns,
>   And all the joys of life with health are flown.

Or, watching while 'Around their dams the sportive lambkins
play' and noticing that 'The voice of music warbles from the
wood, / Delightful objects crowd the smiling scene; / All nature
shares the universal good', the poet sets himself apart in his
dejection: '. . . cold despair exalts no breast but mine' (Graeme,
'Elegy I'). An appeal for quiet unanxious hours is certain to be
rejected; as in Langhorne's 'Visions of Fancy':

> Mirror of life! The glories thus depart
>   Of all that youth, and love, and fancy frame,
> When painful anguish speeds the piercing dart,
>   Or envy blasts the blooming flowers of fame.

And more than once in such poems the moment of despair is
extended into a metaphor for the fate of man, the vanity of
human wishes perceived in a recognition that the process of life
from this moment is a descent into poverty and ill health, a loss of
Eden that God alone can restore. Thus John Scott, in 'Elegy I:
Written at the Approach of Spring':

> O why alone to hapless man deny'd
>   To taste the bliss inferior beings boast?
> O why this fate, that fear and pain divide
>   His few short hours on earth's delightful coast?

And in Robert Ferguson's pastoral elegy on 'The Decay of
Friendship', which was in the volume Dorothy used to console
herself a few weeks earlier after hearing Coleridge's 'Verses to

Sara', the speaker finds himself isolated from man as well as nature by his grief:

> And what avail the thoughts of former joy?
>> What comfort bring they in the adverse hour?
> Can they the canker-worm of care destroy,
>> Or brighten fortune's discontented hour?

★   ★   ★

> For now pale poverty, with haggard eye
>> And rueful aspect, darts her gloomy ray,
> My wonted guests their proffer'd aid deny,
>> And from the paths of Damon steal away.

It should be obvious that few of these poems comprising the spring elegy are significant achievements. Even in these scattered quotations the artificiality of diction, rhyme and sentiment are all too apparent. If any or all of them were 'models' for Wordsworth, they served only to define in the most general way a kind of situation, names for a predicament.

In translating five months earlier the Chaucerian 'Cuckoo and the Nightingale', Wordsworth had tried his hand at finding language for a situation that perhaps was a model for the spring elegists of the eighteenth century. The dream vision in which the two birds debate is set in a May landscape where the sleepless dreamer first finds harmony:

> Meanwhile the stream, whose bank I sate upon,
> Was making such a noise as it ran on
> Accordant to the sweet Birds' harmony;
> Methought that it was the best melody
> Which ever to man's ear a passage won.

The debate itself is conducted in language that very clearly anticipates that of stanzas 5 to 7 of 'Resolution and Independence', especially if the lovers of whom the cuckoo speaks are transformed to poets:

> For lovers, of all folk that be alive,
> The most disquiet have and least do thrive;

> The most feeling have of sorrow, woe and care,
> And the least welfare cometh to their share;
> What need is there against the truth to strive?

In fact, the adverse effects of love are those Wordsworth, using the same sort of vocabulary and some of the same rhymes, will later blame on the poet's imagination:

> For thereof come all contraries to gladness;
> Thence sickness comes, and overwhelming sadness,
> Mistrust and jealousy, despite, debate,
> Dishonour, shame, envy importunate,
> Pride, anger, mischief, poverty, and madness.

Even the briefest comparison makes clear how relevant those exercises the previous winter must have been, how essential they were in helping Wordsworth now to find a mode for expressing subsequent perceptions and feelings. Even the paradox of the imagination's effect on the dialectical moods of the mind was present in the opening stanza of 'The Cuckoo', again of course ascribed to a very literary source:

> The God of Love—*ah, benedicite*!
> How mighty and how great a Lord is he!
> High can he make the heart that's low and poor,
> The high heart low, and bring it to death's door;
> And hard hearts he can make them kind and free.
>
> (MS. version.)

However artificial in tone and traditional in form these poems from Chaucer to Ferguson were, they pointed to a way for composing personal experience that was as far from Dorothy's advice to 'study common things' as it was from Coleridge's example of pouring forth with a minimum of self-criticism and discipline the sufferings of the heart. If Wordsworth, in attempting to resolve the unanswered questions of the Ode, was looking for a mode that would allow more expression than Dorothy's way and more orderly discipline than Coleridge's, the spring elegy must have helped him to discover it. To be sure the 'Immortality' Ode could be included in this category as well, but to point out conventional elements in 'Resolution and Independence' is also to emphasize its uniqueness: the manner in which the conventional subject and situation is transformed into an autobiographical narrative. Wordsworth knew well that a convention of this kind, like an epitaph, was one means by which a poet could 'employ the intervention of the imagination in order that reason may speak her own language earlier than she would otherwise have been enabled to do'. Whether the speaker in most of the spring elegies is called 'Damon' or 'I' is unimportant, and the dreamer in 'The Cuckoo and the Nightingale' is individualized only as a lover old 'and to genial pleasure slow'. But in Wordsworth's poem the speaker continuously identifies himself into independence, creating as he speaks a very particular character. The surfeit of spring elegies in the anthologies that Wordsworth knew suggests that he was fully aware of working in the manner of a late eighteenth-century convention, in form if not diction. But, as Wordsworth would certainly have agreed, it is diction, and all that it implies, that makes all the difference, that enables resolution and independence to be terms descriptive of manner as well as result.

The 'I' of 'Resolution and Independence' is invisible at first, heard but not seen. The scene, a moor on a fine morning after a night of wind and rain (the most recent such morning that Wordsworth could have had in mind was that of April 26th), exists for two stanzas by itself, and first appears as sound rather than sight: birds singing, a stock-dove brooding 'over his own sweet voice', a jay answering the chattering of a magpie. The setting indeed is developed with deliberate slowness: the hare runs races 'in her mirth', but is presented for the sake of the mist its feet raise 'from the plashy earth'. When the speaker asserts his own presence, in stanza 3, it is as an observer oblivious to the phenomena the narrator now insists were there, an observer whose heart was 'employed' by the pleasant season, but who must have—in spite of his rapture—seen the hare, heard the distant waters. Such ambiguities of consciousness, first suggested by the distance between the 'I' who was employed and the 'I' who observed, by the distinction between the scene now and the weather during the previous night, by the distance of the waters, the sounds hidden in but expressed through the woods, already mark the great distance between this poem and any of its antecedents. The limits of the scene that is so sharply focused by the observation of the hare are more tenuous than they seem at first glance, and it is a tenuousness analogous to that of the narrator's own consciousness. The man then, with heart employed, presumably did not hear the waters and the woods, just as he contained unawares the remembrances of the vain and melancholy ways of men. To be innocent, happy as a boy, is to be oblivious of time, of place and of identity—and thus to be unable to imagine another time or another place, to be incapable of historical or geographical memory or anticipation. To be only here, now, is in a sense not to exist at all, and to have had one's identity incorporated into general existence. It does not require 'Tintern Abbey' to remind the reader that such a state is necessarily transient, and perhaps not particularly valuable. However attractive the charms of silence and oblivion he and Dorothy had shared pretending to be 'happy as they who are dead' a few weeks earlier, Wordsworth now rejects this indulgence. To be a part of what one sees is not to *be* at all.

And the impermanence of such moods is simply a fact of existence. The sudden visitation of memory and anxiety 'sometimes chanceth', and the transparent observer is attacked and made opaque by consciousness, by fears, fancies, dim sadness and blind thoughts. As a result the perception of the man then, like that of the man now who narrates the poem, is double: it includes the present (the skylark), the past (a memory of the hare) and the future ('there may come another day to me'). In other words, the observer and narrator are now, for the time being, nearly one. To be a happy child of earth, a blissful creature, is to walk 'far from the world, and from all care'. To be dejected, then, is to be quite directly 'cast down' from the high moment of delight into the depth of retrospection, circumspection, and self-justification.

Responsibility, for the self and for others, is as necessary as genial faith and genial good. The demands of the world, the reciprocal obligations in a society of men and women who 'build for him, sow for him, and at his call love him', can be abandoned for the sake of delight only in fantasy, only by one who would deify himself by his own spirit. To exist without self-consciousness (stanzas 3, 4 and 5 suggest) is as immoral as it is impossible, for it means participating in the self-defeating selfishness of a Burns, a Chatterton, a Ferguson—and probably Coleridge.

A glance at some of the lives of the poets that Wordsworth read at Grasmere helps to clarify this partly articulated attitude toward poetic careers. The poets described in the biographical sections of Anderson's *British Poets* who began youth in selfish gladness and ended it in despondent madness are many. Chatterton, according to his own sister and to Anderson, passed his brief adult life in gloom 'from the time he began to learn'. And Anderson easily blames the melancholy of Michael Bruce (who died at twenty-one) on his literary career:

... he seems to have felt in common with those who possess a genius, of which imagination and feeling are the strongest characteristics, that pensive melancholy, which is ever attendant upon poetical enthusiasm ... [and which is aggravated by being] conscious of rectitude of conduct and unmerited adversity (*BP*, XI, 274).

Morals and medicine combine oddly too in Anderson's assessment of the career of Graeme, who died at twenty-two: 'It is a consideration mortifying to human pride, that fine talents and the most exquisite sensibility are but too often the predisposing cause of an insidious and fatal disease' (*BP*, XI, 418). To be sure this alliance of genius and madness was a biographical cliché, and it would be merely speculative to assert that Wordsworth, because he could have been reading these introductions at this time, necessarily had them in mind. But Dorothy in her *Journal* reminds us that after hearing Coleridge's 'Verses to Sara' she did turn to the life and verse of Ferguson (almost certainly in David Irving's edition of 1800 which was in Wordsworth's library when he died),[1] and the language she found there for Ferguson's short career closely anticipates that of 'Resolution and Independence'. As an undergraduate at St. Andrews, says Irving, Ferguson

[1] *Poetical Works of Robert Fergusson, with the life of the author by* D[avid] *Irving* (Glasgow, 1800).

'rendered himself conspicuous among his brother collegians as a "fellow of infinite jest, and most excellent fancy" ' and 'There is no reason to believe that his natural propensity for mirth and gaiety often caused him to relax in his exertions'. The progress toward despondency (Irving uses the word twice in this connection) is not the result of natural propensity but of adversity, especially the failure of patronage: 'The miseries of a young man of genius and sensibility, who thus found himself upon the vast theatre of human life, without friends to shelter him ["... how can he expect that others should / Build for him, sow for him"] from the storms of adversity, and scarce one ray of hope to brighten his future prospects, may be more easily conceived than described.' Irving, less naively deterministic than Anderson as a biographer, quotes Campbell in locating the beginning of the last stage of Ferguson's madness in a conversation he had with 'a pious Divine, of this sect called Seceders from the church of Scotland' who 'of a sudden joined him' and 'accosted him in a polite and familiar manner'. As they parted, 'the one [was] convinced that he had found a lost sheep, the other that he had been led too far astray, to find favour in the sight of the chief Shepherd of Israel'. It was after this event that Ferguson 'sunk into a state of religious despondency', though previously 'his body was emaciated by disease, and his mind totally unhinged'. Irving, like his Mr. Campbell, is a lively biographer. The encounter with the pious Divine, and the account of Ferguson's sudden moment of perception as he entered the public asylum, are rendered in vivid details that would be hard for a sympathetic reader to forget. Conveyed to the asylum in a chair by his friends, as if he had been about to pay an evening visit, Ferguson reached the building where 'all was wrapt in profound silence':

The poor youth entered the dismal mansion. He cast his eyes wildly round, and began to perceive his real situation. The discovery awakened every feeling of his soul. He raised a hideous shout, which being instantly returned by the wretched inhabitants of every cell, echoed along the vaulted roofs. His companions stood aghast at the dreadful scene: the impression which it made upon their minds was too deep for time ever to efface.

Later biographers of Ferguson remove the mystery by emphasiz-
ing the evils of his Edinburgh life and raising the possibility of
syphilis. Even Irving, when the dramatist is pressed by the
moralist, is willing to grant that evil ways caused the madness and
death. But the remembered effect of his tale is quite different:
despondency, if not madness, appears as the ineluctable fate of the
neglected poet who cannot reconcile his situation to his talents
and ambitions. And terror can be the consequence for a man of perceptive imagination and sensitivity able suddenly to recognize this
incongruity.

Even though Wordsworth mentions only Chatterton and
Burns directly, and surely has Coleridge in mind, a recollection of
Ferguson's fate also lies behind these stanzas on the fate of the
poet, and perhaps even the story of Ferguson's meeting with the
pious divine casts on Wordsworth's memory of the original
leechgatherer he met a year and a half earlier the tone of vague
anxiety that is missing from Dorothy's straightforward account
at the time (3 October, 1800). There is nothing even slightly
sinister in Dorothy's unusually flat factual statements about the
Leechgatherer: 'His face was interesting. He had dark eyes and a
long nose. . . . He had had a wife. . . . He lived by begging. . . .'
Yet in William's poem, and in his comments on it, he insists on the
shock of the meeting, on its distance from an encounter between
ordinary men, and on the unknowableness of what was to follow
from it. 'What is brought forward?' he asks Sara Hutchinson in
his letter of June 14th,

'A lonely place, a Pond' 'by which an old man *was*, far from all house or
home'—not stood, not sat, but '*was*'—the figure presented in the most
naked simplicity possible. This feeling of spirituality of supernaturalness
is again referred to as being strong in my mind in this passage—'*How
came he here* thought I, or what can he be doing?' I then describe him,
whether ill or well is not for me to judge with perfect confidence, but
this I can *confidently* affirm, that though I believe God has given me a
strong imagination, I cannot conceive a figure more impressive than
that of an old Man like this, the survivor of a Wife and ten children,
travelling alone among the mountains and all lonely places, carrying
with him his own fortitude, and the necessities which an unjust state
of society has entailed upon him.

10

The naming of the figure that 'simply *was*' is crucial to the poem. To name it satisfactorily Wordsworth must define the experience in which it appears, and commit himself to a mode for the poem. Is the figure created or observed, is it a part of the landscape's composition or an intrusion of humanity (even society) that makes the world more complex than even the memory, anticipation, and anxiety of the previous stanza had done? A sense of similar mysteries informs Coleridge's 'Verses to Sara' but they exist there without local habitation or name. Here they are just as mysterious—' . . . whether it were by peculiar grace, / A leading from above, a something given . . .'—but they are located and personified: 'I to the borders of a Pond did come / By which an Old Man was, far from all house or home' [early draft]. To find for this appearance a name, or even an order of being, brings to bear all Wordsworth's practice as a maker of epithets and his understanding that to give an epithet to this figure is far more important than finding new names for daisies and cuckoos. No part of the poem received more careful revision that this, for this is the moment within it that decides the poet's relation to his circumambient universe, whether he is to be passive before the apparition, or the author of that apparition who can control it by giving it a history, a dramatic extension in the time and space of his own world, as well as a name.

Lest solitude become isolation, the process of acknowledging is slow, deliberate, careful. Finally, after considerable revision, the figure is said to be like a stone that is like sea-beast that is like 'a thing endued with sense'. In this transformation, the object becomes as familiar and remote and unthreatening as the old woman that crowns the summit of Helm Crag. Coleridge, in an entry made in his notebook for April–May 1802, describes a perception that may have been derived from the poem, but more likely suggested to Wordsworth the form that the transformation might take:

The rocks and Stones put on a vital semblance; and Life itself thereby seemed to forego its restlessness, to anticipate in its own nature an infinite repose, and to become, as it were, compatible with Immoveability.   Kirkstone / (NB, 1189.)

This transformation of human and inanimate, which Wordsworth describes in the 1815 Preface, is an instance of 'the con-
ferring, the abstracting, and the modifying powers of the Imagination, immediately and mediately acting':

The stone is endowed with something of the power of life to approxi-
mate it to the sea-beast; and the sea-beast stripped of some of its vital
qualities to assimilate it to the stone; which intermediate image is thus
treated for the purpose of bringing the original image, that of the stone,
to a nearer resemblance to the figure and condition of the aged Man;
who is divested of so much of the indications of life and motion as to
bring him to the point where the two objects unite and coalesce in
just comparison.

But before the epithets were discovered, and used for mediation,
the figure was more simply a man who 'seem'd like one who
little saw or heard, / For chimney nook, or bed, or coffin meet.'
But even then his life, as a man, is a metaphor of process—'feet and
head / Coming together in life's [earlier, 'their'] pilgrimage'—and
the language still acknowledges no more human life outside the
poet's mind than would a fanciful description of a rock formation,
a motionless cloud, a pond, a construction of which the long grey
staff of shaven wood is as integral a part as the body, limbs and
face it props. Like a landscape, the figure of the man is a collection
of parts that the observer composes and distinguishes at his will,
as Dorothy did looking down from Nab Scar. And the figure's
moving altogether is almost a chance phenomenon, the cloud
that for some reason 'heareth not the loud winds when they
call; / And moveth all together, if it move at all.'
     The encounter, the salutation, the recognition of the Leech-
gatherer as another man is thus postponed for six stanzas after his
appearance, and then only its motion, its assertion of its life,
prompts the poet to speak to, even challenge it:

> And now such freedom as I could I took;
> And, drawing to his side, to him did say,
> 'This morning gives us promise of a glorious day.'

In the earlier versions the figure's reply is postponed by a long
description, later omitted, of his pack and clothing. The salutation,

in both versions, has simply broken the silence, and the significant part of the Leechgatherer's reply is not to be found in his words ('pompous' rather than 'choice' Wordsworth first called them) but in his tone—in the majesty of order and solemnity that emerges from the ambiguous figure, part natural formation (and invested with all that means), part feeble old man. In the earlier versions Wordsworth apparently (to the distress of the Hutchinsons) allowed the Leechgatherer's words to appear in direct quotation. But in revising the poem Wordsworth seems to have acknowledged that the old man's situation and his language are separate in their importance, and the account of his life is reduced finally to a stanza of indirect discourse.

No early manuscript versions of stanzas 17 and 18 survive, but presumably they did not differ greatly from the 1807 version, in which the poet withdraws from the *sense* of the language he hears (. . . his voice to me was like a stream / Scarce heard') into his 'former thoughts' (the 'stream scarce heard' had in fact been literally present as the 'distant waters' of the third stanza). And renewing the question to the Leechgatherer becomes again not an inquiry but an attempt to escape from the memory and anxiety promoted by the passive imagination,

> The hope that is unwilling to be fed;
> Cold, pain and labour, and all fleshly ills;
> And mighty Poets in their misery dead—

by establishing the presentness of this moment, here, now. And this time the words *are* heard, both as sound and substance. Especially in their revised and abbreviated form, the syntax as well as the tone of the words is particularly relevant. Past ('Once I could meet'), present ('But they are dwindled') and future ('Yet still I persevere') are ordered by lines, grammar, and tone. The assertion of confidence in the midst of adversity is a matter of style as well as belief for the Leechgatherer. And because this is— in the rather simplified terms of the old man—an imaginative act, it is relevant to the poet, who begins himself to move from anxiety to perplexity, then to imaginative composition of his own, in the lines that Coleridge praised in chapter 22 of *Biographia Literaria*:

In my mind's eye I seemed to see him pace
About the weary moors continually,
Wandering about alone and silently.

Now at last the Leechgatherer is perceived, apprehended, in all
his perplexing relevance not as a threat, an apparition, an admonishment, or a Doppelgänger, but as an image over which the
poet has control because he invented it. He is accommodated to
the poet's imagination, which in accommodating it also controls
and orders it. The Leechgatherer *tells* the poet nothing—he
becomes something that the poet creates; and in creating, the poet
reaches a sense of equilibrium, of balance and ease. Through the
poet's imaginative act the firmness of mind that the Leechgatherer is *seen* to exhibit becomes communicable. The figure
itself remains decrepit, even somewhat ridiculous, heroic only in
very limited terms—he is a long way from Michael. Nor is this an
instance of Wordsworth breaking through egotistical sublimity
to recognize Otherness, and he does not pretend that it is. His
interest in the old man never deviates from self-concern: 'I could
have laughed myself to scorn to find / In that decrepit Man so
firm a mind.'

The final couplet of the poem, then, is not to be taken in any
sense as a summary or moral. It is a statement earned by the
speaker in the poem, not the poet, and it simply, rather inadequ-
ately, recognizes the distance that has been travelled. Imagination,
acting passively, has subjected the speaker to misery remembered
and anticipated. But the active imagination is the means by
which the discrepancy between present, future and past can be
resolved. The consequence of this resolution is, of course, independence—the ability to act and apprehend independent of the
mind that suffers, by means of the mind that creates. The dialectic
of extremity of experience that informs the beginning of this
poem and the whole of the 'Verses to Sara', dejection itself, is
overcome when in the imaginative perception of solitude is
discovered an independent perception of unity. The authentic
man triumphs in his power and freedom when the perceptions of
the child are reconciled to the contemplations of an adult. The
most appropriate abstract explanation of such a moment perhaps

comes not from Wordsworth, but from Coleridge in his 'Formation of a More Comprehensive Theory of Life'. There man

has the whole world in counterpoint to him, but he contains an entire
world within himself. Now, for the first time at the apex of the living
pyramid, it is Man and Nature, but Man himself is a syllepsis, a
compendium of Nature—the Microcosm! Naked and helpless cometh
man into the world. Such has been the complaint from eldest time; but
we complain of our chief privilege, our ornament, and the connate
mark of our sovereignty. *Porphyrigeniti sumus!* In man the centripetal
and individualizing tendency of all Nature is itself concentrated and
individualized—he is a revelation of Nature! Henceforward, he is
referred to himself, delivered up to his own charge; and he who stands
the most on himself, and stands the firmest, is the truest, because the
most individual, Man. In social and political life this acme is interdependence; in moral life it is independence; in intellectual life it is
genius. Nor does the form of polarity, which has accompanied the
law of individuation up its whole ascent, desert it here. As the height,
so the depth. The intensities must be at once opposite and equal. As
the liberty, so must be the reverence for law. As the independence, so
must be the service and submission to the Supreme Will! As the ideal
genius and the originality, in the same proportion must be the
resignation to the real world, the sympathy and the inter-communion
with Nature. In the conciliating mid-point, or equator, does the Man
live, and only by its equal presence in both its poles can that life be
manifested!

The extent to which Coleridge succeeds in this early attempt to
reconcile a kind of evolution to conventional Christianity is
unimportant here. What is most relevant is the poise and balance
of the statement, based on a double awareness of where man is,
his position as the fulfilment of a general law or process, the 'positive or universal principle in Nature' which diminishes him, and
his independent potentiality, the 'negative principle in every
particular animal' which is 'limitative' of this process because it is
'constantly acting to individualize and, as it were, figure the
former'. As a result, the fully authentic man knows that 'life itself
is not a *thing* . . . but an *act* and *process*'. Both Wordsworth's
Leechgatherer and his speaker find their being, stay secure, in
reconciling act and process by individuation, by using, on very

different levels, what they see around them in order to create
what they become. It is difficult to imagine that Coleridge would
have written this passage of prose without 'Resolution and
Independence' before him, for it expresses the kind of confidence
that is also present when he revised the 'Verses to Sara' as
'Dejection'.

Such philosophical translation is of course more Coleridge's
way than Wordsworth's, but 'Resolution and Independence' is
made more familiar from repeated analogues in *The Prelude* and
The Excursion, for he indeed is the man who at the summit of
Snowdon acknowledges in the power by which he is both
elevated and overwhelmed,

> the express
> Resemblance, in the fulness of its strength
> Made visible, a genuine Counterpart
> And Brother of the glorious faculty
> Which higher minds bear with them as their own.
> That is the very spirit in which they deal
> With all the objects of the universe;
> They from their native selves can send abroad
> Like transformations, for themselves create
> A like existence, and, whene'er it is
> Created for them, catch it by an instinct;
> (1805: XIII, 86–96)

It is particularly appropriate that most of the Spots of Time
where such questions are raised dramatically but unresolved
(e.g. 'unknown modes of being') should have been composed in
the years preceding 'Resolution and Independence' and that this
passage should have followed it. Much of the last book of *The
Prelude* indeed can serve as a commentary on this poem, for its
subject too is almost explicitly the resolution and the independence of those who possess imagination of a high order, who have

> the consciousness
> Of whom they are habitually infused
> Through every image, and through every thought,
> And all impressions; hence religion, faith,

And endless occupation for the soul
Whether discursive or intuitive;
Hence sovereignty within and peace at will
Emotion which best foresight need not fear
Most worthy then of trust when most intense.
Hence chearfulness in every act of life
Hence truth in moral judgments and delight
That fails not in the external universe.

*   *   *

For this alone is genuine Liberty: (1805: XIII, 108–122)

That the search for the meaning of the figure of the Leech-gatherer is the search for this authenticity of the self is made clear more than once by the imagery that orders both poems. To some degree, *The Prelude* is 'Resolution and Independence' writ large in that they both represent a means to the discovery of imagination, or 'clearest insight, amplitude of mind / And reason in her most exalted mood':

... we have traced the stream
From darkness, and the very place of birth
In its blind cavern, whence is faintly heard
The sound of waters; follow'd it to light
And open day, accompanied its course
Among the ways of Nature, afterwards
Lost sight of it bewilder'd and engulph'd,
Then given it greeting, as it rose once more
With strength, reflecting in its solemn breast
The works of man and face of human life,
And lastly, from its progress have we drawn
The feeling of life endless, the great thought
By which we live, Infinity and God.
(1805; XIII, 172–184.)

This talk of streams, of rising and falling, losing and greeting, disappearance and re-emergence in both poems establishes the identity of their concern. The Unknown—the gibbet, a discharged soldier, a Leechgatherer—must be perceived, hailed, named, pursued, and controlled in order for the self to find its location in what might otherwise be endless and meaningless process, if not chaotic hostility. And the control is discovered in the *feeling* of progress, the sense that, as in a vision, the Leech-gatherer's speech set against his pacing 'About the weary moors continually, / Wandering about alone and silently' can be made a part of something that does have meaning.

It is easy to say that these passages in *The Prelude* name more than they dramatize; or that 'Resolution and Independence' dramatizes more than its final preachy couplet can name. Both poems, in very different modes, are attempts both to dramatize and describe the growth of awareness as compensation for the decay of spirit. *The Prelude*'s material is a life seen up to the age of thirty-five, organized somewhat as a narrative. The material of 'Resolution and Independence' is less easy to limit, just as its mode is more difficult to name. Its action takes a few moments in the life of a man just turned thirty-two, but because of the mood of the poet's mind those moments comprehend a life-time. Because of what we know of Wordsworth's activities that spring, we can be even surer that the poem attempts to resolve bio-graphical questions of intense concern that have previously been expressed as abstract lyrics ('The Rainbow'), as lyric descriptions ('To a Daisy'), even as an unfinished philosophical ode. In these poems the asking of questions, and the means for answering them, are circumscribed by the forms the poems take, for in spite of Dorothy's advice, studying common things is a control that also limits. 'To H. C. Six Years Old' (which was written in 1802 and shares with a stanza of 'Resolution and Independence' one of the manuscript sheets sent to Longman in 1807) shows in its slightness how the choice of mode and subject can be a limitation. 'To H. C.' is a kind of protective charm invoking health for Hartley (its prophetic insight, though irrelevant, is interestingly accurate), made necessary by the fear that his exquisite wildness, his apparent but tenuous harmony with the universe make him vulnerable: 'Thou art so exquisitely wild, / I think of thee with many fears / For what may be thy lot in future years.' The possible alternatives are very simple and antithetical:

> Nature will either end thee quite;
> Or, lengthening out thy season of delight,

> Preserve for thee, by individual right,
> A young lamb's heart among the full-grown flocks.

Because the alternatives are simple and antithetical, the poem can either invoke magic ('Bless thee') or end with a series of epithets that preserve though they rename the vague paradox of the future:

> Not doomed to jostle with unkindly shocks,
> Or to be trailed along the soiling earth;
> A gem that glitters while it lives,
> And no forewarning gives;
> But, at the touch of wrong, without a strife,
> Slips in a moment out of life.   (1807 version.)

This portrait, compared with that of Hartley in the finished 'Immortality' Ode, or that of the disillusioned poet in 'Resolution and Independence', shows how much difference a mode makes. Like Coleridge in the 'Verses to Sara', Wordsworth here is hampered by asking the wrong questions. It is the achievement of 'Resolution and Independence' that Wordsworth discovers how to ask a question that can be resolved only by using all the resources of the imagination rather than by a simple act of re-naming, magical or otherwise. What distinguishes the epitaph from the epithet, Wordsworth implies in the essay quoted at the beginning of Chapter I, is the momentary contravention of reason through impersonation. The intervention of the imagination occurs *not* when the poet asks, How do I here see you There (the answer, for the epitaph maker, is, Dead) but rather, How can I imagine myself in a relation to you that makes death (grief, pain, anxiety, loss of sensitivity) irrelevant. Impersonation alone is the means by which 'the survivors bind themselves to a sedater sorrow' and gives licence to the imagination so that 'the reason may speak her own language earlier than she would otherwise have been enabled to do'. Thus what the Leechgatherer *is* leads, ideally, to the question of what the poet's relation to him can become. But in 'To H. C.' or most of the other similar poems before 'Resolution and Independence', impersonation simply does not take place, or takes place on such an easy level (as in 'The

Rainbow') that it is unavailing. Hartley Coleridge remains an object so completely outside the poet that the tone taken toward him is rather patronizing. And Wordsworth there temporarily abandons his own assumption, expressed in the Preface to *Lyrical Ballads* and fully realized in 'Resolution and Independence', that

... it will be the wish of the Poet to bring his feelings near to those of the persons whose feelings he describes, nay, for short spaces of time, perhaps, to let himself slip into an entire delusion, and even confound and identify his own feelings with theirs; modifying only the language which is thus suggested to him by a consideration that he describes for a particular purpose, that of giving pleasure.

The end and effect of this, he says, is to select the words that thus are more than fanciful, that are 'the emanation of reality and truth'.

Perhaps seeing and hearing the almost total failure of impersonation in Coleridge's 'Verses to Sara' led Wordsworth to the discovery of a new mode in 'Resolution and Independence', where every resource of poetry is devoted to such intervention. But clearly the perplexity of events preceding that early May day on which the poem was begun made the discovery necessary and important. The two significant poems that immediately follow 'Resolution and Independence', 'A Farewell' and the 'Castles of Indolence' stanzas, define relationships (between Mary and Grasmere, between Wordsworth and Coleridge) with an ease of impersonation that speaks *from* rather than *for* the sake of resolution, or independence. As in Coleridge's 'Theory of Life', the discovery of sovereignty in man is concomitant, on a social level, with the recognition of interdependence.

CHAPTER V

Afterward

THE OBSERVATION that Wordsworth's poetry after 1802 was gradually damped down into that of a sixty-year-old smiling public man is not the less true for having been made so often. The sovereignty expressed by the Distributor of Stamps for Westmorland in his attack on free public education for women ('. . . hands full of employment and not a head above it, afford the best protection against restlessness and discontent'—speech on laying the foundation stone of the new school in Bowness, 1836), or in his opposition to the extension of the Kendal and Westmorland Railroad on the grounds that the effect of wild nature on the uneducated was meaningless at best, corrupting at worst, is a long way from the sovereignty earned in 'Resolution and Independence'. In 1801 Wordsworth had introduced himself to C. J. Fox as the would-be defender of 'the blessings of independent domestic life'. What he was defending forty years later was a sort of fiefdom, located morally and socially as well as geographically, for which he acted as Guide and Conscience. One of his objections to the railway, for instance, is that the influx of crude travellers and their depraved entertainments ('wrestling matches, horse and boat races without number, and pot-houses and beer-shops') will drive out 'the gentry—whose . . . families have ministered, and still minister, to the temporal and spiritual necessities of the poor, and have personally superintended the education of the children in a degree which does those benefactors the highest honour, and which is, I trust, gratefully acknowledged in the hearts of all whom they have relieved, employed, and taught' (letters to the *Morning Post* in December 1844).

To be sovereign of himself, even of his family and friends, is one thing, but for him to extend this role, unmitigated by childlike enthusiasm or delight, into the public world at large is quite another. Not really begun in gladness, certainly not ending in despondency and madness, the poetic career of Wordsworth does seem to have depended on his momentary perceptions of something more than he could easily resolve. The worry in 'Home at Grasmere' that Town End was not the world ceased, and if people suggested occasionally during his state visits to London that the emperor wore no clothes, he was impervious. Keats, for instance, referred to him as Lord Wordsworth (25–27 June 1818), and elsewhere, with Wordsworth and Hunt in mind, he spoke disparagingly of 'Each of the moderns [who] like an Elector of Hanover governs his petty state, & knows how many straws are swept daily from the Causeways in all his dominions & has a continual itching that all the Housewives should have their coppers well scoured . . .' (3 February 1818).

The poetry Wordsworth wrote after 1802 was not invariably inferior, but like Grasmere and the Lakes it had begun to serve a very different function. Even the *Guide to the Lakes*, unlike *The Prelude*, fails to prepare its reader for the sense of nature's hostility inherent in the sudden deprivation of light in sunless Honister Pass, nor does its tone allow for that sensibility that once called Easedale the Black Quarter. Substantially at peace now with himself and the world he understood and ruled, annoyed and waspish toward any encroachment from outside it, Wordsworth's single-mindedness directed his sensibility elsewhere, and was deflected only occasionally by an event such as the drowning of his brother John ('God keep the rest of us together! the set is now broken.'). The resources of sovereignty and authenticity are used, not questioned or often rediscovered.

In the reply to John Wilson's letter that William and Dorothy spent three days in early June of 1802 preparing, Wordsworth explains quite frankly the psychological purpose for and from which he has written. The poet, he says, should do more than merely reflect faithfully 'the feelings of human nature':

. . . he ought, to a certain degree, to rectify men's feelings, to give them new compositions of feeling, to render their feelings more sane, pure, and permanent, in short, more consonant to nature, that is, to eternal nature, and the great moving spirit of things.

Though this talk of reconciliation is explicitly aimed at over-coming Wilson's aversion to 'The Idiot Boy', Wordsworth could hardly have failed to notice that his language here restates abstractly the resolution achieved in 'The Leechgatherer'. But *composed, consonant, permanent, pure* and *sane* can be the qualities of a vision of permanence, or of boring poetry, the work of a sensibility that no longer need depend upon imagination for its life.

In 'Tintern Abbey' and *The Prelude*, the achievement of a new composition is closely followed by a turn to Dorothy, or Cole-ridge (or in the last book of *The Prelude*, both) to attest to the validity of that which cannot otherwise be dramatized—the Presence, even the 'prime and vital principle' where 'keepest thou in singleness thy state'. In the days that saw the completion of a full text of 'Resolution and Independence', Wordsworth used separate poems for similar shifts of attention. 'A Farewell', the 'Poem on Going for Mary', is of course explicitly about Town End rather than Mary. But the house and garden and view, as 'Home at Grasmere' more openly suggested, are as much equiva-lents for Dorothy as they are places and things. Her ambience as *genius loci* is incorporated into the ambiguous 'we' who speak throughout the poem. On May 29th, the day William finished the poem and Dorothy wrote it out, she carefully inscribed inside the cover of the notebook describing these weeks three names and the date (the names later incompletely obliterated):

~~Mary Wordsworth~~
~~Dorothy Wordsworth~~
~~William Wordsworth~~
Sat Evening
May 29th

And Dorothy's need for tribute and reassurance is further suggested by her accounts of her elegiac mood throughout the early summer. On May 8th an undistinguished line in an un-distinguished anonymous poem in the *Monthly Review* (XXXVII, 328–9) sets her weeping 'For names, sounds, faiths, delights and duties lost'. The fact that the poem *attacks* Cowley for seeking retirement from the world as a form of lotus-eating ('sullen apathy, and sordid rest' on 'Calypso's magic coast'), mourns for his being *less* manly than the unwilling exile who weeps 'as sharp anguish came on memory's wing', Dorothy seems to dismiss as irrelevant. Her concern is for a personal past that William's marriage will force her to leave forever, not the Grasmere she is leaving for a few months. Whether her reading with William of *Henry V* was one occasion for this nostalgia the entry in Dorothy's *Journal* leaves unclear, but it is a temptation to imagine Dorothy's hearing in Hal's wooing of Catherine of France a poignant reminder of William's wooing of Annette.

Dorothy's elegiac mood obviously persisted until they left Grasmere for Gallow Hill. On May 31st, the day Wilson's letter arrived and the day Dorothy copied out what she assumed would be the final version of 'A Farewell', even a broken tooth reminded her of the transitory nature of the peace she had found, and is the occasion for her self-consolation: 'My tooth broke today. They will soon be gone. Let that pass, I shall be beloved—I want no more.' And three days later another line, this time from John Logan's 'Ode written on a Visit to the Country in Autumn', is singled out as 'affecting': 'And everlasting longings for the lost.' This poem, which Dorothy says contains 'many affecting lines', is a mournful commemoration of the passing season, the end of innocent youth, the loss of departed friends, 'all human beauty' blasted by 'cruel fate's untimely wind', and the 'wrath of Nature'.

Reminders of loss came to Dorothy from many sources. Even Aggie Fisher's stoical remark that 'there are many heavier crosses than the death of an Infant' seems to have fed and consoled the mood that brought Dorothy, at the end of that day, to read Milton's 'Il Penseroso' to William. Dorothy's drift toward nostalgia, even despondent self-pity, was presumably deflected by their month with Annette and Caroline at Calais in August, but it obviously reached a point beyond consolation at William's wedding in October. If she has often until now appeared in William's poetry as a source for justification, she rarely appears there after this May even as an occasion for his consolation. Except

for 'A Farewell' and 'The Sun has Long been Set', the poetry
written after 'Resolution and Independence' is marked by its
distance from Dorothy's concerns. The moments of consolation
that Dorothy experiences are extra-literary: On June 2nd, after a
walk to Butterlip How,

> . . . we sate in deep silence at the window—I on a chair and William
> with his hand on my shoulder. We were deep in Silence and Love, a
> blessed hour.

Although the size of the final settlement from Lord Lowther's
estate made Dorothy's financial separation from William less
painful and less necessary than she anticipated, the letter she and
William sent to Richard on June 10th suggests how extensive her
sense of a changing life was. Because of William's marriage, she
says (protesting strongly that no blame for this is to be ascribed to
the marriage), she is 'obliged to set him aside, and I will consider
myself as boarding through my whole life with an indifferent
person'. Independence she accepts with great reluctance. To be
able to 'buy a few books, take a journey now and then', she
tells her lawyer brother, is 'highly desirable that a person of my
age and with my education should have in her power', but the
prospect of such freedom is not welcomed with enthusiasm—the
'principal object' of the request for separate independent mainten-
ance is 'to make me tranquil in my mind with respect to my future
life'. To be sure, Dorothy's tone to Richard is in its usual distant
and testy form—her remarks about Mary and the wedding are
very non-committal and she seems deliberately to avoid mentioning the trip to France—but her anxiety about a bleak future is
unusually clear. In spite of William's exclamation to him on the
death of their brother John in 1805, Richard obviously was never
a real member of the Set, and William's marriage was almost as
shattering to Dorothy's world as a death might have been. The
page of blotting paper facing the entry for May 15th is a commemoration, a blind hope, in other words an epitaph that puts
together the random scribblings inside the covers of the notebook
and stands for the mood behind the relatively composed sentences
of these weeks:

S. T. Coleridge
Dorothy Wordsworth   William Wordsworth
Mary Hutchinson   Sara Hutchinson
William   Coleridge   Mary
Dorothy   Sara
16th May
1802
John Wordsworth

In the repetition of names occurs the very shift so painful to Dorothy. William and Dorothy, like the Hutchinson sisters, cease to form a pair. The second time through, she, like Sara and almost like John, is removed from the centre of the world she was so fond of imagining. She fears that the centre will now be William, Coleridge and Mary.

If the shifting epitaph is an accurate index of Dorothy's private fears, it is misleading about William's literary concerns. In the poems after 'Resolution and Independence' Coleridge is as absent as Dorothy and Mary. To be sure, the stanzas written in Wordsworth's copy of Thomson's *Castle of Indolence* (and imitating its stanzaic form) offer parallel portraits of Coleridge and himself. But both figures are so generalized and stylized that Matthew Arnold can hardly be blamed for mistakenly assuming that Coleridge was the subject of the first four stanzas rather than the last four. Two enormously sentimentalized, sometimes whimsical, figures are juxtaposed, with none of the sense of an encounter between separate identities that marks the appeals to Coleridge in *The Prelude* or that emerges even in Coleridge's maudlin reply to *The Prelude*, 'To William Wordsworth'. In spite of their technical virtuosity, the 'Indolence' Stanzas are surely one of Wordsworth's silliest poems of this year, and their only lively line—the description of Coleridge's 'face divine of heaven-born idiotcy'—was altered before the poem was printed.

What did fully engage Wordsworth's literary interests that May was not an immediate concern with himself, Dorothy, or Coleridge, but with the sonnets of Milton, which Dorothy had been reading to him on May 21st. Dorothy's reading may have encouraged her brother's interest in a literary mode that had not

fully engaged his attention before. Though he does say later that
he knew them all by heart at this time, it was not a form particularly appropriate to the exploratory writing he had been doing.
But the eagerness with which he now took up the composition
of sonnets was more than mere enthusiasm for a new style or a
means of following in the footsteps of greater poets. The sonnets
Wordsworth wrote during the summer of 1802—in their form,
their exclusions, their subjects—serve as an index to a new attitude
toward himself, his poetry, and the world he now saw himself
entering. If with the publication of the second edition of *Lyrical
Ballads* in January 1801, Wordsworth at first proclaimed himself
the poet-defender of 'the blessings of independent domestic life',
the sonnets this summer reflect a growing determination to speak
to a different audience, about different matters. But the change was
slow, complicated, apparently undeliberate. To be sure the only
surviving sonnet from that Friday in May when he began contains
Wordsworth's first reference in a poem to a living public figure:
'I grieved for Buonaparté, with a vain / And an unthinking
grief.' But Bonaparte here is little more than an excuse for using
Milton as a model: talk about public morality and the education
of a Prince is subordinated to concerns as relentlessly domestic as
those of 'A Farewell' (written a week later). In spite of references
to power, battles and the governor, the energy of this poem is
firmly committed to 'motherly' thoughts, womanhood, children,
books, leisure, perfect freedom and 'the talk / Man holds with
weekday man in the hourly walk / Of the mind's business.'
Indirectly the poem reasserts the farewell to ambition of 'Home at
Grasmere', though with less candour and less ambivalence,
perhaps because the prospect of life with motherly Mary seems to
offer fewer confusions than life with sisterly Dorothy.

Most of the sonnets that can be confidently assigned to this
summer are similarly muted, their real subjects somewhat out of
focus, as his daughter Caroline disappears in the sunset of 'It was
a beauteous evening'. The autobiographical intensity of Milton's
'When I consider how my life is spent' is rarely heard, and the
sonnets dedicated to Liberty are, set beside 'The Late Massacre in
Piedmont', oddly abstract and passionless. Indeed, in the later

'Nuns fret not at their convent's narrow room', Wordsworth praised the sonnet because it provided solace and an escape from liberty. Without Dorothy's remark, there would be little reason to emphasize Milton's part in the form or subject of these sonnets (even the first of them introduces an octave rhyme variation that Milton never used). But in their individuality, considered in the light of what else Wordsworth was engaged in that summer, they do appear to be the means of transforming a poetic concern.

Dorothy's *Journal* gives very little sense of the impact that the trip to Calais to see Annette and Caroline must have had on her brother. The sonnets, which in a sense commemorate the stages of that journey, suggest that the impact was considerable. At one point during the return the two records come astonishingly close, and interestingly differ. On August 30th, the day after they had landed again at Dover, Dorothy reports that 'the ... day was very hot. We both bathed, and sate upon the Dover Cliffs, and looked upon France with many a melancholy and tender thought.' The melancholy, presumably, is pity for Annette whose future has now been finally separated from William's and the tenderness is an extension of affection to Caroline who will be irrevocably parted from the father she never knew.

But Wordsworth's sonnet on the same occasion—'September 1802, Near Dover'—presents the English Channel as quite a different sort of barrier, almost 'a lake, or river bright and fair' that sets in 'frightful neighbourhood' the more familiar political climate of England and 'the power', the 'mightiness for evil and good' that the proximity of France affords. The response that Wordsworth describes is fearful—'I shrunk'—and his anxiety is produced not by his past experience but by his sense of an awesome political force that has the energy of blowing winds and rolling waters, an energy that, he implies, is not directed toward freedom because it is not a harmony of the soul with God's 'one decree'. Presumably at this moment William and Dorothy both share anxiety, but the diarist expresses hers in domestic and human terms, the poet in political and religious ones. Rarely do the journals and poems express a greater distance between brother and sister.

Although the sequence of the sonnets, set in the order of the journey to Calais and back, hardly reveals a cause for Wordsworth's new way of regarding his experience, they do reveal a surprisingly clear pattern of change, and set up contrasts within themselves and among one another that can to some extent be defined. As William and Dorothy left England, the words they gave to one of their perceptions are almost identical. Few accounts in Dorothy's *Journal* of things seen are closer to one of her brother's finished poems than her paragraph about crossing Westminster Bridge on July 30th:

We mounted the Dover Coach at Charing Cross. It was a beautiful morning. The city, St. Paul's, with the river and a multitude of little boats, made a most beautiful sight as we crossed Westminster Bridge. The houses were not overhung by their cloud of smoke, and they were spread out endlessly, yet the sun shone so brightly, with such a fierce light, that there was even something like the purity of one of nature's own grand spectacles.

Of course there is some doubt about whether the *Journal* entry preceded the poem (probably not, since the whole account of the trip seems to have been composed several months later when they were back at Grasmere), and Wordsworth himself is rather indefinite about when he actually wrote the sonnet. Whose language came first, however, is not the issue, since both poem and paragraph must recall perceptions they discussed with one another at the time. What is interesting is the ease with which both William and Dorothy accommodate this alien, urban, unusual spectacle— in all its majesty—to a way of seeing they both share, a shared sensitivity to valley, rock or hill. Both accounts admit vague uneasiness—the *fierce* light, the endlessness of houses, the 'mighty heart' that lies still—but their similar metaphors easily contain it.

The shock of France, for William, was not so easy to contain in verse. Caroline, to be sure, is part of a harmonious moment by the sea in 'It is a beauteous evening', but the unexpectedness of this moment is even more transitory and threatened than the one on Westminster Bridge. The nun is breathless with adoration, the thunder of the eternal Being in the sea beats everlastingly, the

child is untouched by thought and in her innocence worships at
'the Temple's inner shrine'. And the other reports of France 'in
the hourly walk of the mind's business' by both William and
Dorothy are even less composed. Dorothy's discontent is, ex-
pectedly, domestic: their lodgings 'opposite two Ladies' are
'badly furnished and with large store of bad smells and dirt in the
yard, and all about'. The weather is hot, Dorothy has a cold and
cannot bathe. Scenes in the countryside may be beautiful, but
Calais itself seems deserted of the light of heaven. Her efforts to
find beauty amid this domestic unpleasantness seem to come
from a determination to be fair-minded in spite of her feelings.

William's terms for his distress, more unexpectedly perhaps,
are not domestic but political. To be sure, reunion with Annette
and a first meeting with Caroline would be unlikely subjects for
an autobiographical poem he might write (even Coleridge did
not expect any references to them in letters), but the dismay
occasioned by France seems actual, not a substitute. On the road
from Calais to Ardres, Wordsworth, remembering his trip there
with Robert Jones in 1790, and hearing again the greeting 'Good
morrow, Citizen', finds the phrase now hollow, 'As if a dead man
spake it'. The attempt to cheer himself up that concludes the
earlier version of the sonnet—'. . . happy am I as a bird / Fair
seasons will come, and hopes as fair'—does not survive in the
other sonnets written in France that month. In two sonnets
especially the bitterness and disillusion are undisguised: the
festival that is merely a name, celebrating Napoleon's birthday
and his life consulship, is contrasted with a 'prouder time' when
'the senselessness of joy was then sublime'; and the English
tourists flocking to France after the peace of Amiens are made
examples of a prostration of mind that is common to both the
English and the French. The creatures of one kind—though sick,
lame, blind, of all degrees—are tasteless in their haste and slavish
in their obeisance to a power that might, for a Frenchman, be
converted to seemly reverence but here is a vulgar offering to new-
born majesty that has arisen 'When truth, when sense, when
liberty were flown'. The cynical use of a metaphor for social
decorum sets a new tone in these sonnets, even in Wordsworth's

verse: 'What hardship had it been to wait an hour' is a sneer, almost a growl, that one might have thought Wordsworth incapable of.

In the sonnet written on his landing again at Dover, Wordsworth tried to recapture the chauvinism of the 'Fair star of evening' which acts as a glorious crest to the 'one hope, one lot, / One life, one glory' that is England. But by now such a moment of undeviating joy in his own country must be deliberately recreated, by exclusions. To be sure, the cock, the curling smoke, the bells, the playing boys, the waves—'all, all are English'. But 'Europe is yet in bonds':

> . . . but let that pass,
> Thought for another moment. Thou art free,
> My Country! and 'tis joy enough and pride
> For one hour's perfect bliss, to tread the grass
> Of England once again, and hear and see,
> With such a dear Companion at my side.

To compose his feelings at the moment of landing obviously requires every sort of resource—attention to the natural, at least impersonal, images of unmodified bliss, the exclusion of political attitudes, finally the consolation of Dorothy's companionship.

Thus far the threats to composure are kept at considerable distance in the sonnets—they are French, or in Haiti and Venice and Sweden, or called Napoleon, or embodied by English tourists in France. England at least seems to be the repository of essential virtue and hope, a place on which one can fix the attention that is so rudely disturbed when it looks elsewhere. But the return to London, with such knowledge of the rest of Europe, brings out attitudes far different from those so easily composed when they crossed Westminster Bridge on the way to Dover, or those which marked their return to British soil. The first sonnet written in London begins with an almost desperate, explicit appeal for help:

> O Coleridge! [MS.] I know not which way I must look
> For comfort, being, as I am, opprest,
> To think that now our life is only drest
> For show; mean handy-work of craftsman, cook,
> Or groom!

England, after all, is like France a country where 'The wealthiest man among us is the best', and where 'rapine, avarice, expense' have replaced peace, fearful innocence, and 'pure religion breathing household laws' as objects of adoration and obedience. It was during this three-week stay in London (at Montague's rooms in the Temple) that the city took on for Wordsworth the nightmare qualities expressed with such energy in book VII of *The Prelude*. On September 7th, William and Dorothy dined with Charles and Mary Lamb, who had just returned from a visit to Coleridge at Keswick and to the Clarksons who had been living in the Wordsworths' cottage. After dinner, the Lambs took the Wordsworths through Bartholomew Fair (held from September 3rd to the 7th), the event which becomes, in early 1804 when Wordsworth resumed work on that part of *The Prelude*, the 'blank confusion! and a type not false / Of what the mighty City is itself'. The details—the learned pig, the stone eater, chattering monkeys and albinos—were obviously recollected from this visit with the Lambs in 1802, and the point made about them in 1804 appears in lines that Wordsworth had been working toward since he wrote 'Michael' at the end of 1800. The fair becomes a type, an epitome, a strange reality for the confusion rather than the corruption of civilization. Here, as in the lines written in MS. J of *The Prelude* years earlier, the danger is that a man in such a world may lose his ability to distinguish,

> Living amid the same perpetual flow
> Of trivial objects, melted and reduced
> To one identity, by differences
> That have no law, no meaning, and no end.
> (1805: VII, 701–4.)

The cry to Coleridge for help in the first London sonnet after his return does not of course incorporate much beyond a vague sense of this 'anarchy and din'. But in retrospect it is quite clear that Wordsworth found in London that summer something he was impelled to talk about, for which he could not yet find an adequate form. And Lamb, who loved it all, can hardly have been much help.

The road out of what Wordsworth saw as a hell of grimacing, writhing, screaming humanity eventually took several forms. By the time he wrote book VII of *The Prelude*, of course, he recognized that in recreating hell he has himself ordered it, for

> . . . though the picture weary out the eye,
> By nature an unmanageable sight,
> It is not wholly so to him who looks
> In steadiness, who hath among least things
> An under-sense of greatest; sees the parts
> As parts, but with a feeling of the whole.
>   (1805: VII, 707–12.)

To make connections and contrasts, to find syntax and verse for such a spectacle, of course enables Wordsworth in *The Prelude* to move rather easily on to the contrasting Helvellyn Fair with which book VIII begins, and a celebration of domestic and filial harmony, where

> immense
> Is the Recess, the circumambient World
> Magnificent by which they are embraced.
>   (1805: VIII, 46–8.)

Bartholomew Fair, which in a sociologist's terms might be called the hideous product of a deracinated urban mass culture, becomes in the sequence of *The Prelude* the simple obverse of a spontaneous, pastoral popular culture, if the observer is a man who has learned to know the difference by a 'feeling of the whole'.

But the London of *The Prelude* was a composed, reflected upon, resolved version of what Wordsworth must have seen and felt in September 1802. The London in these sonnets is still an abstract hell, and the way out equally unrealized. He appeals to Coleridge (who of course had spent much of the previous winter in London), and then to Milton. What the fen of stagnant waters needs is a man with a soul like a star (an echo of 'Fair Star of Evening') and a voice like the sound of the sea, and a man who dwells apart. What Milton (or Coleridge) is expected to do is unclear: he is to 'raise up', to 'give us manners, virtue, freedom, power' and magically replace the inward happiness that has vanished from altar, sword, pen, fireside, hall and bower. Both heroic and saintly, he must be a rescuer and redeemer, poet, priest and patriot. Like the Great Men in the sonnet that probably followed the one to Milton, Milton represents a spirit that is more political than literary:

> These moralists could act and comprehend:
> They knew how genuine glory was put on;
> Taught us how rightfully a nation shone
> In splendour: what strength was, that would not bend
> But in magnanimous meekness.

And the most likely source for such a revolutionary spirit, modern France, has become instead of the birthplace of heroes and new ideas,

> Perpetual emptiness! unceasing change!
> No single volume paramount, no code,
> No master spirit, no determined road;
> But equally a want of books and men.

Wordsworth's literary ambitions when he went north to Gallow Hill on 22 September 1802 seem to have changed considerably from when he had left Grasmere two months before. The sonnet about Bonaparte on May 21st was dedicated to the virtues of domestic tranquillity, the ones in September bring into far closer conjunction the vocation of poet and public man, and virtue has now found a more public task for itself. Dorothy's premonitions about the increasing distance between her world and that of her brother have more than the impending wedding to justify them. For two months, in the constant company of Dorothy, revisiting some of the most significant people and places from his own past, Wordsworth seems to have found a vocation that makes irrelevant much of that sense of the past that gave energy to most of his important poems from 'Home at Grasmere' to 'Resolution and Independence'. Now the emergence of places and public events as primary concerns for poetry can only mean that people, domestic relations, and self-justification are far less compelling motives for composition. Not until the end of the year did he return to work on *The Prelude*, and much of the best of that poem had already been written.

Dorothy's account of the wedding of William and Mary at

Gallow Hill on October 4th, and of the return of the three of
them to Grasmere, is the most extensive sustained narrative in the
Journal—full of candid self-revelation and pervaded by her fear
that she no longer knows or fully understands the brother with
whom so much of this year has been spent. Her account of
William's giving her the wedding ring to wear the night before
the ceremony and of her helpless retreat to her bedroom next
morning when the two men come 'to tell us it is over' expresses
both the joy of intimacy and the pain of its loss. She makes every
effort to include Mary in terms similar to those William used for
her in 'A Farewell' (she is 'our dear Mary'), but the parallels between this trip back to Grasmere and the one she and William had
made in December 1799 'after we were left to ourselves' are
obviously more painful to Dorothy than to her brother. In the
tone of her description of their dinner at Leyburn 'where Wm
and I had dined with George Hutchinson . . . 2 years and 3/4 ago'
there is restrained resentment: '. . . while the rain beat against the
windows we ate our dinners, which M. and W. heartily enjoyed
—I was not quite well.' From October to the end of the year,
after their return to Grasmere, she is careful to notice who takes
walks with whom, and where Mary is when she is alone with her
brother. Finally, on Christmas Eve, 1802:

William is now sitting by me, at 1/2 past 10 o'clock. I have been
beside him ever since tea running the heel of a stocking, repeating some
of his sonnets to him, listening to his own repeating, reading some of
Milton's, and the *Allegro* and *Penseroso*. It is a quiet keen frost. Mary is
in the parlour below attending to the baking of cakes, and Jenny
Fletcher's pies. Sara is in bed in the toothache, and so we are [?]. My
beloved William is turning over the leaves of Charlotte Smith's
sonnets, but he keeps his hand to his poor chest, pushing aside his
breastplate. Mary is well and I am well, and Molly is as blithe as last
year at this time. Coleridge came this morning with Wedgwood. We
all turned out of Wm.'s bedroom one by one, to meet him. He looked
well. We had to tell him of the birth of his little girl, born yesterday
morning at 6 o'clock . . .

If this sounds almost like Dorothy's accounts of the domestic
tranquillity at Town End a year earlier, she seems to have taken

less and less pleasure in describing it. No domestic journal by her survives after this one ends in January 1803, and Dorothy's failure to keep it up between November 8th and Christmas (and again between Christmas and January 11th) suggests that no entries were written, in spite of her resolutions. Perhaps significantly, the journal of the tour to Scotland recorded weeks when Mary was absent.

The return of Coleridge to the north on that Christmas eve in 1802, when Dorothy informed him of the birth of his daughter Sara, was for him but a temporary suspension of a series of journeys that had kept or would keep him away from Keswick much of the autumn and winter of 1802-3. In August he spent a week by himself on a walking tour of Westmorland and Cumberland which included an energetic ascent and terrifying descent of Scafell. November and December he spent mostly in Wales with Thomas Wedgwood. By January 20th he would be off again—for Etruria, Bristol, Stowey, Gunville (Dorset) and London—until April.

But at some time in the summer of 1802, between July and September, Coleridge applied himself to poetic composition, as both subject and activity, with more consistent diligence than he had shown in many months. His notebooks and letters frequently discuss poetry (his, Wordsworth's, poetry in general); he planned a volume of essays on modern poets; and his political journalism and translations seem to have been activities necessary to sustain a serious writer in doing his own work, rather than escapes from it. But more important, during the summer he wrote the 'Hymn before Sunrise' and thoroughly reshaped as a very different sort of work the 'Verses to Sara' he had written the previous April.

The dates of these two compositions are obscure, partly because Coleridge seems to have been deliberately misleading about the origin of both poems. The 'Hymn before Sunrise', for instance, he described to Sotheby in September as having 'poured out' spontaneously 'in the manner of the Psalms' during his ascent of Scafell in August, with the scene changed to Switzerland only because English mountains seemed too humble to sustain the significance he was ascribing to them. But he does not tell Sotheby that Frederike Brun's ode in the manner of Klopstock ('Chamouny beim Sonnenaufgange') was at least as important to his poem as either the Psalms or his experience as a mountain climber. With a similar lack of candour, the 'Verses to Sara' when quoted in letters become verses to Wordsworth or Poole, although Coleridge rather coyly alludes to the more personal passages he omits in transcribing them. If Wordsworth's palpable design in his letters is to keep alive his reader's interest in him as a poet, Coleridge was not above using his poetry to provoke his reader's interest in him as suffering man, and his remarks about his own work tend to be intensely personal, and usually misleading. The most interesting of his literary activities during the summer—the revision of the 'Verses to Sara' and the changed sense of himself as poet that went into the composition of the 'Hymn before Sunrise' —he simply does not mention.

The letter of July 29th to his brother-in-law Southey is an excellent example. He begins by describing the circumstances of the Wordsworths: they should get £5,000 as a result of the Lonsdale settlement, William will return from Yorkshire 'in about a month *one of us*' (that is, married—though Coleridge knew that with the visit to France the wedding would be at least two months away). Then he describes as virtually finished a book on the Greek testament controversy, another on tythes, a third that would be an anthology of modern poets with an accompanying volume of commentary. Then, apparently thinking of the contrast between Wordsworth's productive spring and his own, he mentions the fact that Wordsworth has written thirty-two poems but that they are marred somewhat by a 'daring humbleness of language and versification, strict adherence to matter of fact, even prolixity' that has been brought about by Wordsworth's failure fully to understand the conversations with Coleridge that lay behind the revised Preface. As so often before, a comparison with Wordsworth leads Coleridge almost inevitably to imply his own superiority in understanding and to profess his inferiority in talent:

As to myself, all my poetic Genius, if ever I really possessed any *Genius*, & it was not a mere general *aptitude* of Talent, & quickness in Imitation is gone—and I have been fool enough to suffer deeply in my mind, regretting the loss—which I attribute to my long & exceedingly severe Metaphysical Investigations— & these partly to Ill-health, and partly to private afflications which rendered any subject, immediately connected with Feeling, a source of pain & disquiet to me.

Coleridge is, of course, paraphrasing the 'Verses to Sara', the terms of which have now become for him an unquestioned equivalent for his experience, and he goes on to quote from the poem toward which he has been subtly moving. But if he had before him the April text, the fair copy with few revisions headed 'To—, April 4, 1802' preserved now at Dove Cottage, he was rewriting the poem as he quoted it. As in the letter to Sotheby ten days before, he regards the poem almost as a series of fragments, capable of being moved about and put into new relations with one another. A first large step toward the composition of the ode called 'Dejection' is made: he quotes the passage beginning 'There was a Time when, tho' my Path was rough' to illustrate the point he has just made in prose, but in the process 'Ill Tidings' (the lost letter from Sara) have become 'Afflictions' and Coleridge says he has omitted 'a dozen Lines that would give you no pleasure' (actually the twenty-two lines describing the 'habitual Ills ... when two unequal Minds / Meet in one House, & two discordant Wills' and the absence there of any sympathy, grief, enjoyments or hopes in his 'coarse domestic life' that would provide the 'Fair forms & Living Motions' his heart could borrow to mourn for Sara). As in the final versions of 'Dejection', then, the poem now moves directly from the account of the loss of the shaping spirit of imagination to the infection of the soul caused by abstruse research.

This letter to Southey ends with Coleridge's hopeful description of the improved relations between himself and his wife, and further talk about how life at Greta Hall could be reorganized to allow the Southeys to live there. Throughout the letter Coleridge *talks* as though there were no difference between the poem and his life as it might be described to a friend, and in sending the verses to Sara he of course speaks to her first as a lover, then as a poet. But what he has now *done* is to use the poem also as an artifact, a series of lines that can be re-arranged to suit a subject as well as an audience. For instance, the meaning of the lines about abstruse research, because of their changed context, is quite different, and far more general in its application. For all his talk to Southey about himself, Coleridge has begun to reshape 'Dejection' as a poem about imagination rather than as a gesture of love and an appeal for pity.

The revising of the 'Verses to Sara' that took place between the end of July and the publication of 'Dejection' in the *Morning Post* on Wordsworth's wedding day, October 4th, is partly a matter of exclusions such as this one in the letter to Southey, partly an attempt to take advantage, through a complex and demanding formality, of the changes in meaning and tone that such exclusions cause. The stanzaic form, implicit here and in other letters when Coleridge also isolates fragments to quote, changes drastically the relation between reader and poem. Anyone looking at the manuscript of the 'Verses to Sara' is all too conscious of being a rather alien intruder at a moment of private confession. It is almost possible to indulge the fantasy that the blots on the page are tear-stains. But even a superficial reader confronting the carefully constructed and numbered stanzas of the Ode is reassured, by form at least, that he is in the presence of something as old as the Greeks and timelessly formal: a work of art not an event in life.

As critics have always pointed out, this revision is in no simple sense an 'improvement'. The 'Verses to Sara' are often confusing, and at many points the alien reader can move from one line or stanza to the next only by imagining what Coleridge might have felt as he wrote. The reader's sole resource, in other words, is often his ability to postulate a character who might say such things. If the reader were Sara Hutchinson or Southey or even Sotheby, his understanding depended on his intimacy with the writer, and presumably his difficulties were relatively few compared to those of a reader today who must create a whole milieu, the minor characters as well as the speaker.

But given all that Coleridge says about himself in letters and notebooks, and all that his articulate contemporaries have said about him, it would have been possible to imagine a man who was dependent on the full realization of feeling in his domestic life with wife and children in order to find forms for expressing his more private feelings of sympathy for someone like Sara Hutchinson, who is not only outside his domestic existence but felt to be a threat to it. The incompatibility between what Coleridge *sees* to be the integrated and harmonious life of the Wordsworth circle and *experiences* as the fragmented deadness of his own family leads, he says, to a kind of speechlessness to which the only alternative is metaphysical research where imaginative activity is less dependent on the feeling of emotional wholeness. But the effect of this impersonal speculation, in turn, is to cut him off even more permanently from the moments of emotional stress on which any sort of resolution and integration depends, and from the dream, almost fantasy, of harmony that his love for Sara might sustain. Unable to give—that is, to feel sympathy or sorrow or joy spontaneously—he is thus unable to receive the benefits of and consolations for such emotions. Many lives replace and exclude the One Life, which ought to have been the dowry of a new Earth and new Heaven. The final image of Sara as a conjugal and mother dove borrowing genial warmth from those she warms is thus the perfect image for that integrity from which he is excluded. Indeed the very fragmentary and uneven pace of the long poem itself expresses the isolation of experience into ambivalent moments.

However, the difficulties of the final Ode and the means available to a reader for overcoming them are very different. The 'person' addressed ('Wordsworth' in July, 'Edmund' when the poem was published in the *Morning Post*, 'Lady' in *Sybilline Leaves* and after) becomes increasingly abstract, more and more like a muse and less like a cause. For the first three stanzas of 'Dejection' the difference between poem and letter is not extensive or crucial. But stanza IV of the Ode takes an entirely different direction. In the letter the statement about giving and receiving life follows almost 250 lines of analysis, complaint, memories, introspection and dreams. It is, there, a conclusion. In the Ode, however, it is a postulate, an assumption for which the reader is to expect no dramatized explanation. We are asked to read the rest of the Ode having first granted the existence of the One Life, and thanks to the vagueness and generality of the statement, it offers no particular obstacles—it is the sort of proposition familiar enough in most philosophical or romantic poetry. The assertion about the One Life is really an introduction to its more familiar name, Joy, and when he uses the word in stanza V (l. 64), Coleridge states the subject of the poem by completing the antithesis set up by having used 'Dejection' as its title. The word 'dejection' never appears in the 'Verses to Sara' (though Coleridge used it twice in his letter to Sotheby on July 13th), and 'Joy' does not appear in this weighted sense until line 314. In the letter 'Joy' acquires meaning gradually as it is used in a variety of contexts ('the Joy within me dallied with distress' or 'My little Children are a Joy, a Love'), and the sudden insistence on the word at the end is a matter of discovery and resolution. But in the Ode the word is introduced early as a significant concept, and its subsequent appearance in less insistent contexts reminds the reader that this is not a simple noun about a state of feeling, but a spirit, a power, a voice, a luminous cloud, the source of the One Life.

In the Ode, statements about the past (as in stanza VI) are made within the context of a general proposition about life, and are not stages in a process of discovery. Thus the sole resource of abstruse research is as an antidote to the loss of imagination's shaping spirit; Reality's dark dream has no clarifying antecedent (in the 'Verses' its antecedent was his 'dark distressful dream' of Sara's sickness during his absence); and the act of paying attention to the wind's mad lutanist is not the forcible replacing of one fantasy with another, but an act of literary composition to counter the more abstract philosophical analysis that has preceded it. In effect, the speaker at this point in the Ode says, 'I can still write in a variety of styles' not as in the earlier version 'I can force myself not to think about Sara'.

In the text published in the *Morning Post*, this process of altering meaning by excluding referents is even more obvious. There, in fact, the poem moves directly from 'My shaping spirit of Imagination' to 'O wherefore did I let it haunt my mind, / This dark distressful dream' (omitting even the lines about the sole resource of abstruse research). But at the time Coleridge obviously still thought of this as an edited poem, not a rewritten one, for the text in the *Morning Post* at this point has three lines of asterisks, and a note saying that 'the Sixth and Seventh [are] omitted'. Thus the stanzas finally numbered VII and VIII are numbered VIII and IX (stanza IV was later divided). At the time 'Dejection' appeared in the *Morning Post*, Coleridge was not yet confident of the new meanings his text had acquired.

The eighth (or, in the *Morning Post*, ninth) and last stanza of the Ode, here as in the 'Verses' a prayer, is the only place in the revised poem where the person addressed, Sara, Wordsworth or The Lady, had any reality (she sleeps, she has eyes and a voice), and the final blessing has a rather decorous, almost chaste, dignity about it. The Lady could be almost anyone, and is addressed in such a way that her anonymity seems entirely appropriate. In the *Morning Post* version, where the person blessed is of course not Sara or Lady but Wordsworth (called Edmund), the slightly patronizing remark about 'simple spirit' is expanded by six lines to give him literary rather than maternal qualities, and the speaker pays tribute to him as a poet:

> With light heart may he rise,
> Gay fancy, cheerful eyes,
> And sing his lofty song, and teach me to rejoice!
> O EDMUND, friend of my devoutest choice,
> O rais'd from anxious dread and busy care,
> By the immenseness of the good and fair
> Which thou see'st everywhere,
> Joy lifts thy spirit, joy attunes thy voice,
> To thee do all things live from pole to pole,
> Their life the eddying of thy living soul!
> O simple spirit, guided from above,
> O lofty Poet, full of life and love,
> Brother and friend of my devoutest choice,
> Thus may'st thou ever, evermore rejoice!

If no one can know when Coleridge first conceived the notion of having the poem published on Wordsworth's wedding day, it is tempting to imagine that this was the motive for revising it so thoroughly. William and Dorothy of course were familiar with its first form as a letter to Sara, and they would know by how far the revisions exceeded a simple substitution of names. Ironically, the date itself had a significance that William and Dorothy, if not Mary, must have known: October 4th was the Coleridge's seventh wedding anniversary. Though Coleridge may have taken a macabre pleasure in the coincidence, he never revealed it, and the Wordsworths never mentioned it. A more generous interpretation can be given to the coincidence of dates: for Coleridge on that day to publish a poem born in the misery of his own marriage but revised in such a way as to suppress if not control much of its original self-pitying tone was a gesture for which William and Dorothy must have felt some admiration. And Wordsworth would inevitably see the new poem not just as a tribute to him and his work in general, but as a reply to 'Resolution and Independence', which he had been reworking from May to July. Indeed Coleridge's lines describing Wordsworth as having been 'raised from anxious dread and busy care / By the immenseness of the good and fair' seem an explicit allusion to that poem. 'Dejection' in the *Morning Post* version is as much a poem to and about Wordsworth as the one Coleridge wrote in reply to *The Prelude* in 1805: it is a poem addressed to a fellow poet about the experience of having written the 'Verses to Sara' and then realizing, after hearing 'Resolution and Independence', what more a better poet could do in combating dejection. All the maudlin envy of the letter is gone, to be replaced by respectful admiration, and it is the greater austerity of style in the Ode, more than the explicit tribute at the end, that makes it a generous wedding present.

A year and a half earlier, when Coleridge told Godwin that 'the Poet is dead in me', he implied that the discovery was caused by a number of recognitions for which he could not yet compose any order. His failing health and the discord at Greta Hall obviously were involved, partly because he consequently felt the necessity of turning his mind to abstruse research where he would be less perturbed by personal feeling (or the awareness of its absence). Yet the drift toward abstraction was only partly voluntary. His notebook entries for March of that year repeatedly describe situations in which immediate perceptions—of a wall, for instance, or light reflected from a tumbler—vanish and are replaced by involuntary images or sensations from inside: '— abstract Ideas— & unconscious Links!!' He even set four-year-old Hartley worrying about the difference between the prospect of mountains seen directly through the window and the same scene reflected in a looking glass. 'Tintern Abbey' is very much in his mind as he speculates about the relations between observing objects and observing the self, at the same time that he writes to Godwin that his biographer ought to record that 'Wordsworth descended on him, like the [Know Thyself!] from Heaven; by showing him what true Poetry was, he made him know that he himself was no Poet'.

Interests similar to those of the spring dominate the letters, note-books and poems of the late summer and autumn of 1802, with the difference that they are now parts of a more articulate, if equally upsetting, order. The difficulties of poetic composition in the midst of domestic discord are set out of course in the 'Verses to Sara', and lie behind the lines he revised for 'Dejection', as his use of the poem in his letters shows. Writing to Wedgwood on his own birthday in October, after some accommodations between husband and wife have been worked out to ease the last weeks of her pregnancy, he thanks the Wedgwoods that he has been able to reach the age of thirty, and rather gratuitously describes the pain-ful scenes that had followed his return to Keswick in March:

Scarce a day passed without such a scene of discord between me & Mrs. Coleridge, as quite incapacitated me for any worthy exertion of my faculties by degrading me in my own estimation. I found my temper injured, & daily more so; the good & pleasurable Thoughts, which had been the support of my moral character, departed from my solitude—I determined to go abroad—but alas! the less I loved my wife, the more dear & necessary did my children seem to me. I found no comfort except in the driest speculations—in the ode to dejection, which you were pleased with, these Lines in the original followed the line—My shaping Spirit of Imagination . . .

Coleridge then goes on to quote the same twenty-odd lines he had omitted from the letter to Southey in July, describing the house

inhabited by unequal minds and discordant wills, but he also tells
Wedgwood that circumstances had improved by the end of the
summer.

Nevertheless, a month after this letter to Wedgwood, Coleridge
still seems unable to keep from hurting his wife: first by spending
a day at Penrith with Sara Hutchinson; then by ascribing the
difference between himself and her to his own reliance on inner
life, hers on outer ('the Eye & the Ear are your great organs');
finally by excusing all these previous offences in terms Mrs.
Coleridge must have found fatuous:

Had there been nothing but your Feelings concerning Penrith I should
have passed it over—as merely a little tiny Fretfulness—but there was one
whole sentence of a very, very different cast. It immediately disordered
my Heart, and Bowels. . . . My bodily Feelings are linked in so peculiar
a way with my Ideas, that you cannot *enter into* a state of Health so
utterly different from your own natural Constitution—you can only
see & know, that so it is. Now, what we know only by the outward
fact, & not by sympathy & inward experience of the same, we are
ALL of us too apt to forget; and incur the necessity of being *reminded*
of it by others. And this is one among the many causes, which render
the marriage of unequal & unlike Understandings & Dispositions so
exceedingly miserable. Heaven bear me witness, I often say inly—in the
words of Christ—Father, forgive her! she knows not what she does. . . .
My dear Love! let me in the spirit of love say two things / 1. I owe
duties, & solemn ones, to you as my wife; but I owe equally solemn
ones to Myself, to my Children, to my Friends, and to Society. . . .

As this letter shows, the relations between husband and wife now
were not much less exacerbated than they had been a year earlier,
but they were, at least on Coleridge's part, stated with far less
ambiguity. His terms for co-operation in changing their 'mere
Cat-Hole into a Dove's Nest' are unambiguous: because Mrs.
Coleridge is his inferior 'in sex, aquirements, and in the quantity
and quality of natural endowments whether of Feeling, or of
Intellect', she cannot presume to tell him how he shall behave
toward his friends (as a mother loves many children, so a man
cannot love one wife exclusively), but he may advise her about
hers. And Sara Coleridge can hardly have been pleased by her
husband's hope that Sara Hutchinson, of the three women then

at Grasmere, will come in to attend her during her confinement so that his wife will have a chance to know and appreciate her better. But at least Mrs. Coleridge can have had no doubts about where she stood.

The passivity and abstraction that Coleridge seems sometimes to have chosen as defences and sometimes regarded as afflictions were also given far more articulate literary form during this summer. If in 'Dejection' he dramatizes his inability to write in a Wordsworthian mode, 'A Hymn before Sunrise' represents the sort of lesser poetry he thought he could successfully compose. During his August walking trip in the mountains he had had, he says, an alarming experience during his descent from Scafell. Imagining himself at one moment 'crag fast' on a ledge, unable to go forward or back, he lay down and (he wrote next day to Sara Hutchinson)

was beginning according to my Custom to laugh at myself for a Madman, when the sight of the Crags above me on each side, & the impetuous Clouds just over them, posting so luridly & so rapidly northward, overawed me / I lay in a state of prophetic Trance & De- light— & blessed God aloud, for the powers of Reason & the Will, which remaining no Danger can overpower us! O God, I exclaimed aloud—how calm, how blessed am I now / I know not how to proceed, how to return, but I am calm & fearless & confident / if this Reality were a Dream, if I were asleep, what agonies had I suffered! what screams!—When the Reason & the Will are away, what remain to us but Darkness & Dimness & a bewildering Shame, and Pain that is utterly Lord over us, or fantastic Pleasure, that draws the Soul along swimming through the air in many shapes, even as a Flight of Starlings in a Wind. . . .

The state he describes and the language he chooses for it perfectly balance (and perhaps confuse) passivity and individual re- sponsibility, although his words certainly lack the clarity of the 'Theory of Life' passage quoted in Chapter IV above. He is literally a prisoner of his environment (though he may be exaggerating for Sara's sake, since he did not mention the incident in his very detailed notes of the journey and his discovery of a way out seems rather too fortuitous). And his consciousness too is passively receptive—lying back, he is in a trance. Yet the trance is the mode through which he escapes the terror of his predicament, and he finds expression for it in a hymn of praise to rationality and the human will. In some ways the situation is analogous to that of 'This Lime-Tree Bower' or 'Frost at Midnight', but in both these earlier poems space and time are in effect transcended by 'swimming sense' or 'the idling Spirit'. Here an explicit, if unclear, distinction is made between the passivity of a *prophetic* trance and the mindlessly passive state of a starling driven by the wind, or a man's life dominated by a search for pleasure or the agony of a dream.

Though Coleridge undoubtedly confused readers deliberately by alluding to this experience on Scafell and ignoring his reading of Frederike Brun in describing the genesis of the Hymn, he did attempt to make a poem that would incorporate passivity and an appreciation of impersonality as virtues. In the version of it that appeared in the *Morning Post* on September 11th, the mountain (Mont Blanc now rather than Scafell because it seemed more appropriate to such loftiness) acts as intermediary between the voices of nature (the rushing waterfalls, sighing pine woods, bursting ice, singing meadows), and their creator. Its permanence and silence make it an ideal ambassador, and its physical form of course joins Heaven and Earth. As the speaker steadily gazes at it, the silent mountain disappears as a topographical object and becomes a form, a manifestation of the Invisible.

> Around thee, and above
> Deep is the sky, and black: transpicuous, deep,
> An ebon mass! Methinks thou piercest it
> As with a wedge! But when I look again,
> It seems thy own calm home, thy crystal shrine,
> Thy habitation from eternity.
> O dread and silent form! I gaz'd upon thee,
> Till thou, still present to my bodily eye,
> Did'st vanish from my thought. Entranced in pray'r,
> I worshipp'd the INVISIBLE alone.

Then somehow, mysteriously, like the shadow of the ship in the 'Ancient Mariner' or the flickering flame in 'Frost at Midnight', the mountain in overwhelming its perceiver makes him suddenly articulate. Apparently becoming more like the natural voices, a human one under such influences can awake and address its God:

> But I awoke, and with a busier mind,
> And active will self-conscious, offer now
> Not, as before, involuntary pray'r
> And passive adoration!—
>
> Hand and voice,
> Awake, awake! and thou, my heart, awake!
> Awake ye rocks! Ye forest pines, awake!
> Green fields, and icy cliffs! All join my hymn!
> And thou, O silent mountain, sole and bare,
> O blacker, than the darkness, all the night,
> And visited, all night, by troops of stars,
> Or when they climb the sky, or when they sink—
> Companion of the morning star at dawn,
> Thyself Earth's rosy star, and of the dawn
> Co-herald! Wake, O wake, and utter praise!

A part of, yet able to command, the natural scene, the speaker is a psalmist, the poem has become a hymn, and self and society both disappear. As the announcement of a literary mode, the 'Hymn before Sunrise' is not particularly exciting (or for Coleridge very different from what he had done often enough before). Much of its significance, at this point, must lie in its being Coleridge's admission of what he can *not* do—his implicit surrender in the lingering competition with Wordsworth.

Presumably, as George Watson has recently argued[1], it was Coleridge's innovation and proficiency in what he called the Conversation Poem that first showed Wordsworth the literary possibilities of a poem addressed to an intimate audience, which he exploited so successfully in 'Tintern Abbey' and in most of his subsequent poems until 'Resolution and Independence'. After all, in 1795 when Coleridge had written 'The Aeolian Harp' Wordsworth was still working on such poems as 'Guilt and Sorrow', an imitation of Juvenal (Satire VII), and translations from Catullus.

[1] George Watson, *Coleridge the Poet* (London, 1966), pp. 61–9.

'This Lime-Tree Bower', 'Frost at Midnight' and 'The Nightingale' all preceded 'Tintern Abbey'. But a comparison of the 'Hymn before Sunrise' even with Wordsworth's first attempt shows how 'Tintern Abbey' creates far more complex relations between perceiver and perceived and dramatizes a far more subtle encounter with an external universe that incorporated both the personal past and the sense of society that Coleridge in the Hymn dismisses. Never does Wordsworth depend on such a facile relationship between man, God and creation in order to reach a resolution like that of the Hymn, though Coleridge, from 'The Aeolian Harp' on, kept conventional religious assumptions close at hand to use when necessary to solve literary dilemmas. But if 'Tintern Abbey' shows how much Wordsworth had learned from Coleridge in 1798 about the mode of the conversation poem, the easy conclusion of the 'Hymn before Sunrise' shows how little Coleridge in turn could learn from his pupil. In revising the Hymn for subsequent publication in fact Coleridge carefully muted some of his certainties (the voices of nature are *implored* to speak rather than described as speaking), but he never really succeeded in making it a very convincing account of anyone's experience, and perhaps his insistence on calling it a hymn suggests that he did not want it to be.

Unlike most of his major contemporaries (Byron is obviously an exception), Coleridge never fully trusted his ability to transform personal experience into public poetry. For his few obviously successful attempts to do so, such as 'Frost at Midnight', his label 'Conversation Poem' is a partial deprecation. The versions of 'Dejection' are Coleridge's most deliberate attempts to do what Wordsworth had managed in 'Resolution and Independence', and the fact that all the versions are finally inadequate (the 'Verses to Sara' unsatisfactorily private, 'Dejection' itself mystifyingly allusive) demonstrates his inability to compete in the terms he had himself introduced. Very gracefully, the publication of 'Dejection' addressed to Wordsworth on his wedding day is Coleridge's public recognition of the difference between them.

On 13 August 1803, just before he set off for Scotland with William and Dorothy, Coleridge copied out 'Resolution and

Independence' for Sir George and Lady Beaumont. Then he began copying his own 'Dejection' for them, still as a poem addressed to Wordsworth. But by the time he reached the passage describing the suspension of his shaping spirit of imagination he found the task of reciting his own words too much for him:

I am so weary of this doleful Poem that I must leave off. . . . I have been very ill—& it is well for those about me, that in these visitations of the Stomach my Disgusts combine with myself & my own Compositions—not with others or the works of others.

At this point, perhaps, the literary careers of Wordsworth and Coleridge finally become explicitly distinct. Not since their collaboration on the early *Lyrical Ballads*, of course, had there been much acknowledged sharing of goals and styles and ambitions, but until the end of 1802 neither poet seems to have written much without the other poet in mind, and both wrote with constant awareness of the society they, Dorothy, and the two Hutchinson sisters had created. In the 'Verses to Sara', Coleridge had expressed, among other things, his envy of and resentment toward that society and blamed his exclusion from it on his own domestic discord. Revising the poem as 'Dejection' and addressing it to Wordsworth was an attempt to make this sense of exclusion less private, more literary, by making the poem a celebration of a kind of imaginative talent he could appreciate if not share. Its publication on October 4th, then, was an acknowledgement of the differences in their talent and prospects, personal, social and literary. Both he and Dorothy throughout the preceding months had begun to realize that they could never again be as they were— and the trip to Scotland which Coleridge abandoned after two weeks seems in retrospect to have been their vain attempt to recapture a sense of solidarity, making believe that something among them could be sustained in spite of Mary, in spite of Coleridge's lack of direction and flagging poetic ambitions, in spite of William's discovery the previous summer that he could and would sustain himself resolutely and independently. But it was probably several years before it became clear to all of them that Coleridge's failure to be a Wordsworthian poet freed his enormous talents for literary criticism and for other modes of verse, while Wordsworth's enormous success in composing as magnificent poetry the disparate elements of his personal concerns left him little more of permanent interest to address himself to, or anyone in his immediate circle who could care sufficiently.

Both Wordsworth and Coleridge discovered the limits of 'communication' through poetry. Perhaps for the reasons I have suggested, among others, Coleridge could not convince himself that language would bear the responsibilities he wanted to give it. 'Dejection' became wearying to the man who wrote it because it was not magic, could not evoke joy or any other emotion in its author except the ones he brought to it. Nor apparently in any of its versions did it change significantly his relations to the members of its immediate audience: the Wordsworths, Sara Hutchinson. Coleridge used the poem, then, much as he used literary fragments from other writers, as a way of illustrating autobiographical statements in his letters. Often Coleridge's main motive for writing seems to have been to have something to quote from, and his critical consciousness is rarely more than a few moments away from the poetic trance, as his preface to 'Kubla Khan' shows most directly. His fascination with the goings-on of his own imagination usurped most of his interest in the writing of poetry, but only a very narrow view would insist that this was a tragedy for literature.

By suggesting that Wordsworth's achievement in 'Resolution and Independence' was a discovery of self-confidence, a composition and transformation of his own anxieties, I have also implied that it was the difficulty of composing these energies that gave life to most of his earlier poems, and that his success there deprived most of the subsequent poems of any cause to be. Whether this was in fact a matter of cause and effect, it is true that dependence on a responsive audience, especially on Dorothy, became less obvious in Wordsworth's art. Having once thought he was addressing the People when he was in fact speaking to a small, intimate and responsive group of individuals who cared deeply what he said, Wordsworth seems to have discovered in 1802 how essential that intimacy had been, but the discovery once made did not have to be repeated because now he felt himself the centre of the circle they formed. Although he never says so, 'Resolution and Independence' was Wordsworth's assumption of full responsibility for the world he could create. But then, confidently assuming that *all* worlds were as easily addressed as the one he both created and lived in, he found the writing of poetry all too easy. Almost anything then could pass the vague standards of his critical conscience, and partly because of coincidental circumstances— the withdrawal of both Coleridge and Dorothy as constant listeners and their replacement by the uncritical Mary—there was no one outside himself to assert new standards. The ultimate and central critic in Coleridge—the Know Thyself that descended on him was within, with or without Wordsworth's presence—told him where responsibility lay. The external critics on whom Wordsworth depended left him alone, disastrously.

In the autumn of 1803 Coleridge clearly saw the change occurring in Wordsworth's attitude toward composition, but with his persistent loyalty to his own belief in Wordsworth as a great philosophical poet, and without the advantage of hindsight, Coleridge described the change as a salutary one:

I am sincerely glad, that he has bidden farewell to all small Poems— & is devoting himself to his great work—grandly imprisoning while it defies his Attention & Feelings within the sacred Circle & Temple Walls of great Objects & elevated Conceptions.—In these little poems his own corrections, coming *of necessity* so often, at the end of every 14, or 20 lines—or whatever the poem might chance to be—wore him out —difference of opinion with his best friends irritated him / & he wrote at times too much with a sectarian Spirit, in a sort of Bravado.—But now he is at the Helm of a noble Bark; now he sails right onward—it is all open Ocean, & a steady Breeze; and he drives before it, unfretted by short Tacks, reefing and unreefing the Sails, hawling & disentangling the ropes.—His only Disease is the having been out of his Element—his return to it is food to Famine, it is both the specific Remedy, & the condition of Health (*NB*, 1546).

Even without finishing *The Recluse*, Wordsworth seems to have freed himself from the necessity of correction, the irritation at the response of his best friends. But the noble bark was sailing

under the flag of the Public, which provided—eventually—a
great deal of admiration but very little of the anxious, sympathetic,
intimate concerns of his own circle.

The legend of the Lost Leader who sold revolutionary principles
for public acclaim is the melodramatic political model for this
change. But that the change in Wordsworth was literary as well
as political or sociological is shown extensively by his revisions of
The Prelude, intensively by his eagerness to substitute 'humblest' for
'meanest' at the end of the 'Immortality' Ode, lest a party of tourists
get the wrong impression of his attitude toward the sacredness of
Nature. These examples are extremes, and come from the end of
Wordsworth's life, but they show what it means to have gained
a public and lost an audience.

In describing these events biographically, I am of course aware
of other ways I might have chosen in order to reach the same
conclusions. The sociology of literature, especially, provides a
scheme within which the efforts of Wordsworth and Coleridge to
find significant voices seem to be interesting if futile attempts to
compensate for what they both early recognized as the deliberate
exploitation of a mass of readers by producers (writers, journalists,
publishers), who tried to turn those readers into consumers who
could be taught to 'need' that which was most profitably produced. The thesis of Q. D. Leavis' *Fiction and the Reading Public*
and its successors, in fact, is almost contained in two sentences
from the 1802 Preface to *Lyrical Ballads:*

> ... a multitude of causes, unknown to former times, are now acting
> with a combined force to blunt the discriminating powers of the mind,
> and, unfitting it for all voluntary exertion, to reduce it to a state of
> almost savage torpor. The most effective of these causes are the great
> national events which are daily taking place, and the increasing accumu-
> lation of men in cities, where the uniformity of their occupations
> produces a craving for extraordinary incident, which the rapid com-
> munication of intelligence hourly gratifies.

If Wordsworth (or Coleridge) fully realized the implications of
such a charge, the emphasis in the Preface on the naturalness of
diction is not so very odd. The *Lyrical Ballads* were no less than
an effort to define popular culture and propose it as an alternative

to the old evil and the new: the legislative attempts by the con-
servators of aristocratic tastes, and the standardizing of vulgar
tastes that the manufacturers of mass reading promoted out of self-
interest. Like most subsequent efforts to curb the effects of the
profitable arts, *Lyrical Ballads* of course persuaded only the converted, and in so far as they encouraged imitators they damaged
the cause.

Wordsworth's later dissociation of himself from the interests of
that first idealized audience is attested to both by the remarks
surviving from Grasmere neighbours and by the tone of the
Guide to the Lakes and many of the later poems. Too aware after
the publication of *Lyrical Ballads* (especially the second edition)
that interest in spontaneous popular culture could not be imposed
from above or without, both Wordsworth and Coleridge spent
years writing poems and essays accommodating their disillusionment. For Coleridge the shift to another sort of audience was a
matter of deciding to be an educator. His lectures in Bristol and
London assumed that an understanding of the role of literature in
civilized life could be taught, to the sophisticated at least. His *On
the Constitution of the Church and State*, finally, gave to a newly
idealized body of intellectual and educated readers a political role
as well, as the centre of conscience and moral power in a hier-
archical community. If literature could not survive effectively
among the people, an ideal clerisy educated by poetry as well
as politics could exercise power within a new State.

But Wordsworth, whose political interests seem always to have
been immediate and pragmatic rather than theoretical or prophetic,
quickly lost touch with his audience when it failed to applaud his
early efforts. In the 1802 Preface, the Poet, that 'rock of defence
for human nature', was the one who

In spite of difference of soil and climate, of language and manners, of
laws and customs: in spite of things silently gone out of mind, and
things violently destroyed ... binds together by passion and knowledge the vast empire of human society, as it is spread over the whole
earth, and over all time.

By 1815 this ideal but vague audience bound together by poetry
was defined more carefully, but in a manner that made it even

less accessible. The Public, no matter how large, was separated from the People, and summarily dismissed:

The voice that issues from this Spirit [of human knowledge], is that Vox Populi which the Deity inspires. Foolish must he be who can mistake for this a local acclamation, or a transitory outcry—transitory though it be for years, local though from a Nation. Still more lamentable is his error who can believe that there is anything of divine infallibility in the clamour of that small though loud portion of the community, ever governed by factitious influence, which, under the name of the PUBLIC, passes itself, upon the unthinking, for the PEOPLE. Towards the Public, the writer hopes that he feels as much deference as it is entitled to; but to the People, philosophically characterized, and to the embodied spirit of their knowledge, so far as it exists and moves, at the present, faithfully supported by its two wings, the past and the future, his devout respect, his reverence, is due.

Although his last remark in this 1815 supplementary essay—his hope that the reader will find that the poems 'extend the domain of sensibility for the delight, the honour, and the benefit of human nature'—echoes the educational optimism of the earlier Prefaces, its effect is destroyed by what has preceded it. Wordsworth, finding no adequate alternative to the intimate devotion of his immediate circle, finally convinced himself that its lack was to his credit: the virtue of his art was that it was addressed to the People. But they, 'philosophically characterized', did not exist.

Coleridge abandoned art to become a teacher; Wordsworth addressed himself to a fantasy that supported his self-esteem. The social role of poets and poetry in the last century and a half is anticipated as neatly by the divergence of the careers of these two men as it was by their confluence.

Select Bibliography

Among many studies particularly pertinent to this discussion are, for Coleridge:

HAROLD BLOOM, *The Visionary Company* (New York, 1961), pp. 216–23.

BEVERLY FIELDS, *Reality's Dark Dream: Dejection in Coleridge* (Kent State University, 1967).

R. H. FOGLE, 'The Dejection of Coleridge's Ode', *ELH*, XVII (1950), 71–7.

HUMPHRY HOUSE, *Coleridge* (London, 1953), pp. 133–41.

H. M. MARGOLIOUTH, *Wordsworth and Coleridge 1795–1834* (London, 1953), pp. 85–127.

MARSHALL SUTHER, *The Dark Night of Samuel Taylor Coleridge* (New York, 1960), pp. 119–51.

GEORGE WHALLEY, *Coleridge and Sara Hutchinson and the Asra Poems* (Toronto, 1955).

GEOFFREY YARLOTT, *Coleridge and the Abyssinian Maid* (London, 1967), pp. 203–79.

for Wordsworth:

F. W. BATESON, *Wordsworth: A Reinterpretation* (London, 1954, rev. edn. 1956), pp. 146–74.

HAROLD BLOOM, *Visionary Company*, pp. 160–6.

A. E. M. CONRAN, 'A Study of Wordsworth's *Resolution and Independence*', *PMLA*, LXXV (1960), 66–74.

ALAN GROB, 'Process and Permanence in *Resolution and Independence*', *ELH*, XXVIII (1961), 89–100.

GEOFFREY HARTMAN, *Wordsworth's Poetry 1787–1814* (New Haven, 1964), pp. 200–3, 266–73.

G. W. MEYER, '*Resolution and Independence*: Wordsworth's Answer to Coleridge's *Dejection: an Ode*', *TSE*, II (1950), 49–74.

MARY MOORMAN, *William Wordsworth: A Biography* (Oxford, 1957), esp. I, 459–589.

W. W. ROBSON, 'Wordsworth's *Resolution and Independence*', *Critical Essays* (London, 1966), pp. 124–34.

LIONEL TRILLING, 'The Immortality Ode', *The Liberal Imagination* (New York, 1950), pp. 129–59.

JONATHAN WORDSWORTH, *The Music of Humanity* (London, 1969).

Index

Anderson, Robert: importance of *British Poets* to W, 22–4; on mad poets, 129

Arnold, Matthew, 36

Bartram, William: *Travels* quoted by C, 69

Bateson, F. W.: on W, Dorothy W and Mary Hutchinson, 29, 30, 58

Beaumont, Sir George and Lady: C copies out *Resolution and Independence* and *Dejection* for, 170–1

Bonaparte, 148, 151, 155

Bronowski, Jacob: quoted, 4

Bruce, Michael: 129, read by Dorothy W and Mary, 23; quoted, 124

Brun, Frederike: C's use of *Chamouny*, 158

Bruno, Giordano: C copies out ode, 74

Burns, Robert: and *Resolution and Independence*, 107, 129, 131

Byron, George Gordon, Lord, 170

Calais: described by Dorothy W, 151

Campbell, Thomas: *Pleasures of Hope* read by W and Dorothy, 22

Chatterton, Thomas: and *Resolution and Independence*, 107, 129, 131

Chaucer, Geoffrey: W's translations from, 23, 26–9; *Manciple's Tale*, 26, 27–8; *Prioress' Tale*, 28–9

Clarkson, Thomas and Catherine: relation to W and Dorothy W, 22, 25, 79, 103, 123

Coleridge, Samuel Taylor: on writing as composition and communication, 1–2, 3–4, 67–8, 72, 73, 74, 76, 98, 102, 103, 104, 111, 132–3, 140–1, 169, 173; on W, 3, 64, 66, 67, 69–70, 134–5, 136, 158; and W compared and evaluated, 4–5, 171–6;

demands and influence on W, 20, 147, 169–70; plans for emigration, 20, 24–5, 70, 71, 75–7, 91, 93; illness, 69, 70, 71, 75, 77, 78, 81, 106, 159, 164; despondency, 75, 81, 91, 159, 164; relation to Mrs. C and domestic unhappiness, 77, 79–81, 91, 116, 159–60, 161, 164–7; response of W and Dorothy W to C's unhappiness, 78–9; attitude toward his children, 81; notes on Davy's lectures, 88

WORKS

Ancient Mariner, 1, 35, 38, 95, 168

Christabel, 70

Day Dream, A, 96, 116

Dejection (see also *Verses to Sara*), 3, 5, 159–65, 171, 172

Friend, The, 64, 102

Frost at Midnight, 95, 168, 170

Hymn Before Sunrise, 157, 167–70

Kubla Khan, 172

Mad Monk, The, 101

Nightingale, The, 170

Ode to Rain, 25, 78

Ode to Tranquillity, 84–5

On the Constitution of the Church and State, 175

Picture, The, 116–17, 118

Theory of Life, 136, 167

This Lime-tree Bower, 96

To William Wordsworth, 93

Verses to Sara (see also *Dejection*), 67, 69, 73, 76, 80–1, 93–107, 108, 109, 111, 116, 123, 124, 132, 135, 137, 140–1, 157, 158

—— Sara Fricker (Mrs. S.T.C.), 165–7

Cowley, Abraham: quoted by Dorothy W, 144–5

Cuckoo and the Nightingale, The: 26, 29; and *Resolution and Independence*, 125–7

Davy, Humphry: C discusses plans with, 72, 75–6; lectures at Royal Institution, 85–90
Duns Scotus: read by C, summer 1801, 77

Empson, William: on W, 7, 41

Fenwick, Isabella: 27; notes on *Resolution and Independence*, 123
Ferguson, Robert: relation to *Resolution and Independence*, 107, 124–5, 126, 129–31
Fox, Charles James, 17, 142

Gilbert, William: notes to *The Hurricane* quoted by W, 2
Godwin, William: correspondence with C, 24–5, 69, 72, 76, 78, 90–1, 164–5
Graeme, James, 124

Hartman, Geoffrey, 43n
Hobbes, Thomas, 77
House, Humphry: on C Notebooks, 98; on *Verses to Sara*, 102
Hume, David, 77
Hutchinson, Mary (later Mrs. W): visit to Grasmere 1801–2, 25–6, 78; W's decision to marry, 29–31, 58; as subject for *To the Daisy*, 115; wedding, 155–6
—— Sara: C's attachment to (see also C's *Verses to Sara*), 91–2; *Sara's Poets*, 7n, 85

Jonson, Ben, 7, 8, 24, 93

Keats, John: on C, 4; *Fall of Hyperion*, 16; on W, 143

Lamb, Charles: on 2nd edn. *Lyrical Ballads*, 18; visited by C in 1801, 81; on C and *Morning Post*, 83; host for W in London 1802, 153
Langhorne, John, 124
Lawrence, D. H.: on fiction, viii
Leavis, F. R.: on W, 7

Leavis, Q. D.: ref. to *Fiction and the Reading Public*, 174
Lloyd, Charles: quarrel with Ws, 21
Locke, John, 77
Logan, John: quoted by Dorothy W, 145
London in 1801–2: seen by Lamb, 82; by Southey, 82; by W, 82, 152; by C, 82, 89–90
Lowther, Sir James (later Earl of Lonsdale): estate settled, 123, 146

Manning, Thomas: correspondence with C. Lloyd, 21
Milton, John: *Paradise Lost*, 11, 12; *Il Penseroso*, 145, 156; sonnets, 147–9; as potential hero for W, 154–5
Monthly Review: quoted by Dorothy W, 144–5
Moorman, Mary, 25 and n
Morning Post: C's work for, 78, 82, 83–5

Newton, Sir Isaac: C attacks as passive mind, 72

Plato: C on *Parmenides* and *Timaeus*, 84
Pliny: C quotes on revision, 106

Quillinan, Dora (Wordsworth), 27

Rush, Sir William: W's visit to, 22

Saint-Évremond: quoted on solitude, 16
Scafell: C climbs, 167–8
Scott, John, 124
Shakespeare, William: *Henry V* read by W and Dorothy, 145
Smith, James: on W and suffering, 17
Southey, Robert: C's correspondence with, 79, 158–9; on Davy, 90
Spenser, Edmund: W reads, 26, 30; W and Dorothy read *Protholamion*, 119
Spring elegy: and *Resolution and Independence*, 94, 124, 127